I

© 2020 Andy Frazier

All rights reserved. This book or any portion thereof may not be reproduced or used in any manner whatsoever without the express written permission of the publisher, except for the use of brief quotations in a book review.

Version: 1.1a
Release date 1st February 2020
Revised 24/03/2022

Apology.

The cover of this book has been revised to a picture of the record priced Angus bull. The previous cover photo was of Hollywood actors Fred MacMurray and his wife Jean Haver, and I would like it known that at no point were they implicated in this story.

Sotheby's Auction House, London, England. 1974 ........................ 5
PART I ............................................................................................ 6
Connecticut, USA - 1950............................................................. 7
Brooklyn, New York - 1951.........................................................14
Bayonne, New Jersey - 1955 .....................................................22
Downtown Manhattan - 1959 ...................................................33
21 Club, Manhattan - 1959........................................................39
Downtown Manhattan - 1960 ...................................................44
Cornell College, Ithaca, New York - 1961 ...................................48
Chicago stockyards - September 1961 .......................................51
PART II ......................................................................................... 63
Wappingers Falls, New York State - 1961 ..................................64
Attorney's office, Manhattan - Jan 1962...................................68
Wappingers Falls - March 1962 ..................................................70
Sotheby's Auction House, New York - June 1962 ......................73
Wappinger Falls Ranch - May 1962 ...........................................75
Perth, Scotland - February 1963 ................................................80
Newhouse, near Glamis Castle, Scotland - February 1963 .........87
New York Supreme Court - April 1963 ......................................96
New York International Airport - May 1963 ..............................98
Wappingers Falls Ranch - July 1963 .........................................102
Williamsburg, Brooklyn - Fall 1963 ..........................................106
Governor's Office, Birmingham, Alabama, June 1963 .............110
Auburn University Veterinary School, Alabama -October 1963  112
Wappingers Falls - January 1964 .............................................117
Perth auction mart, Scotland - February 1964 ........................119

The State office, South Carolina - February 1964 ..................... 121

Black Watch Arabian Horse stud - September 1964 ................. 123

Lawyers office, New York - July 1964 ........................................ 127

Black Watch Farms - October 1964 ............................................ 129

Highway 97, New York - June 1965 ............................................ 140

Wappingers Falls Ranch - August 1965 ...................................... 142

Sotheby's, London - September 1965 ........................................ 147

Staunton, Virginia - October 1965 ............................................. 151

Wappingers Falls - 1966 ............................................................ 154

Las Vegas - September 1966 ..................................................... 159

Federal Bank, Wappingers Falls - Feb 1967 .............................. 164

Art Gallery, Soho, London - December 1966 ............................ 166

Wappingers Falls Ranch - July 1967 .......................................... 168

Christies auctions, London - December 1966 ........................... 170

Sotheby's Auction House, London - January 1967 .................... 173

Black Watch Farms - July 1968 ................................................. 176

Pottstown, Pennsylvania - Fall 1967 ......................................... 178
PART III ..................................................................................... 181

Dunnellen Hall, Greenwich, New York - July 1968 ................... 182

21 Club, Manhattan, New York - February 1969 ...................... 186

Dunnellen Hall, Greenwich - November 1969 .......................... 190

Greenwich Village, New York - 1971 ......................................... 193

The Anvil Club, 14th Street, New York - 1971 .......................... 196

Dunnellen Hall - 1973 ............................................................... 199

Greenwich Village, New York - September 1973 ...................... 203

Sotheby's Auction house, London - January 1974 .................... 206

21 Club, Manhattan - January 1974 .......................................... 208

Prologue ................................................................................... 210

| | |
|---|---|
| **Final word** | 213 |
| **Facts** | 213 |
| **The Author** | 214 |
| **Acknowledgements** | 214 |

## Sotheby's Auction House, London, England. 1974

'Do I hear two hundred thousand? Come on ladies and gentlemen, who will give me two hundred thousand pounds? Paintings of this quality by Stubbs don't come this way very often. Especially not 'Goldfinger.' Come on now, you know this is a golden opportunity........thank you Sir.' A fleeting sense of relief lit the auctioneer's face.

'Two hundred I am bid....'

# PART I

## Connecticut, USA - 1950

'How old are you, son?'

'Turned 18 last birthday, Sir.' Underneath his clipped smile the teenager's heart was pounding as he rolled out this little lie. It wasn't that lies scared him or even bothered him at all, but more the excitement of the anticipation that a half-truth could be delivered with such confidence and aplomb that it sounded far more credible than the truth itself. And that truth itself was that Jack wasn't eighteen at all – but he was on the run!

'You look kinda strong enough. Have you ever worked cattle or sheep before, boy?

Now was the time to deliver at least *some* real facts. That was the thing about lying, you had to make a judgement about whether you would get caught or, in this case, caught out. With a crooked finger the old farmer pushed his hat back on his forehead, running a half-crippled hand down the side of his weather beaten face as he stared at the short skinny kid in front of him.

'No Sir,' came the reply after a few seconds. 'No Mr Jarvis, I ain't done none of those things, but I am prepared to learn if you give me a chance.' Jack fixed his eyes on the man, locking him there for a brief moment, waiting for the weakness. And then it came, a fraction of a movement in the man's pupil that showed a tiny sentiment towards his seducer. Jack pounced on his opportunity like a fox on a jackrabbit.

'Sir, if you would give me a chance, I can work for free until I have proved my worth.' He let the words hang in the air, his smile dropping into expectancy.

That was it. How could that man, or any man for that matter, refuse such an offer? Free labour from a strong lad? It was a gift, a one-way deal from which a hard-pressed old farmer could never lose. That's all it took. Selling was about giving gifts. Early life in Brooklyn had taught him that much. School had taught him too. Give someone what they want and they'll take it without seeing the price. It had stood him in good stead so far and, as the man's vexed expression morphed into a half-smile, Jack knew it had worked again. As the old farmer reached out his hand, Jack grasped it, showing the gratitude it deserved.

He now had a job.

Ignoring the ground rules that his new employer was laying down, blanking out the detailed aftermath now the deal was closed; he glanced around him, taking in the rural surrounds. It wasn't quite the idyllic station that he had dreamed of during those darker troubled nights. No picket fence or tree lined avenue up to the house; no symmetrical cow-barn or even hog-pen at the entrance. The buildings, such as they were, appeared worn and tired, like an extension of the old farmer himself. But it was a farm nevertheless and more over, miles from anywhere – and that is just where this fifteen year-old wanted to be right now. OK, Connecticut wasn't the other side of the world from New York but it was far enough out into the wilds not to be found or even found out. Let's face it, an hour on a bus could have taken him to way too many places for people to look. School authorities would hand the responsibility back to his parents and they would blame each other until they ran out of ideas. Not that he believed his family really cared that much. His father was too busy with his business to have listened to Jack's problems and his mother, well, he guessed that she would care more about slights to her social standing from her son's disappearance than the fate of the boy. They would get along just fine without him. Mother could revile the youth of today, blaming everyone in the world except herself while accepting the conditional offers of sympathy from all and sundry. Meanwhile, here he would be doing something a little more meaningful than learning math and science from the teachers he despised and carried little respect for.

No, Jack would be just fine here, amongst the cattle, sheep and chickens, in the great outdoors. It seemed that life had just begun. His mind honed back in on to what the old man had been saying. 'You listening to me, boy?' That was another gift that Jack felt he had been presented with in life, that of hearing many conversations while his mind was elsewhere.

'Yes, Sir. The chicken shed. Got it. Cleaning eggs until the sheep-shearers arrive next week. If I break any eggs you will kick my ass...'

'No..I'll kick your too-smart skinny ass! You eat in the bunkhouse. And a one week trial. If you're any use, you'll get ten bucks a week after that. If not, you're back out that'ta gate faster than an old gobbler turkey on a promise.' His eyes lightened as he stared at the boy again. 'I will be watching you. Now get yourself down there, before I change my mind.'

'Thank you, Sir.' Jack nearly added that compared to a physics class with Professor Herman, tending livestock would be a breeze, but kept his mouth closed. Instead he added, 'I won't let you down, Sir,' picking up his bedroll and wandering off towards the old clapperboard barn.

Over the next few days and nights, he listened and learned from the two old farm hands, both who teased him at first about being a city boy with piano player's hands. It wasn't until they sat down around the old potbelly stove one night keeping away the cold that they learned from close experience that those hands weren't just for playing piano, as he cleaned them out at poker.

Taught by his father, Jack had an uncanny knack for card games of all sorts – his head did numbers real well. Numbers worked for Jack, he loved them, finding comfort in the way they flowed, mixed, always gave him an answer. In fact, he found that he had to let the other guys win a hand or else they wouldn't play with him at all. On one occasion, Sam Dogado, a giant Basque sheep-shearer with the McClusky outfit that came every spring to shear sheep at old man Jarvis's place took extreme offence at having most of his hard-earned pay-packet cleaned up in an hour by a punk kid. He picked Jack up by the throat shaking him until he nearly passed out. After that, Jack took a bit more care over how he played people, learning a valuable lesson that, if you are going to take money off folks, at least have the courtesy not to grin in their face as you do so.

Within a week, young Jack got his first taste in the saddle, hauling himself up on to a young bay mare that had far more energy than he probably required for his first fist at playing cowboy, while the two older farmhands leant on a rail and watched on. It was less than thirty seconds before the boy hit the dirt, and just one second more when the men howled with laughter, spooking the bay further. Brushing the dust from his denims, he caught the mare and took her around the other side of the barn, out of sight, determined to master it. Over the next few hours, Jack learned a lesson he would never forget. Getting the better of people was all about looking, learning, pretending and talking; and none of those in isolation worked on animals - they needed trust in the mix as well and that was something that didn't come easily for Jack Dick.

By noon, he had changed horses to a much older dun gelding that was quiet and content to school a young greenhorn with no horse sense.

The cattle on the Jarvis place where a mix of bad

Herefords and Randall Linebacks an old-fashioned breed the family had kept for years. Old man Jarvis regularly cursed them as being, 'No good for nothing save shitting and somewhere for worms to live.' But he didn't seem inclined to make any improvements. Even Jack could see they were a pretty sorry looking bunch when he spent an hour moving them to another 20-acre paddock that didn't contain a whole lot more grass than the bare ground they'd been moved from.

The old dun made Jack feel good and ride tall in the saddle as it ambled along behind the motley looking herd. For a moment he was lost, riding out on a far distant western plain fighting weather and hardships, herding a bunch of Texas Longhorns. He was brought back to his senses by an explosion of cow shit from the rear cow in the herd plastering his horse and him in green manure.

The idea of farming still excited him, but it wouldn't be like this. He would never be that old man in his beaten up clapperboard house, or those worn out farm hands, scratching out a living. No, his would be a grand estate, like they got on the films; with quality horses and fat cattle, and even fatter profits.

Over the next few months, Jack took his pay with the other men three times his age and some, stashing it away in a fine leather saddlebag that he had won in a card game and now kept hidden in the barn. While he was moving the cattle one day his eagle eyes had seen a glint of silver on the ground and he jumped down to inspect it. Picking up the round object, he noted it was a dime dated from some seventy years earlier, a keepsake he would treasure forever. It too found itself in the saddlebag. All his young life Jack had been keen on collecting things. Stamps, coins, pieces of china, he had amassed some of each, passionately wondering about their heritage and beginnings. In the evenings, he would sit and roll the coin across his knuckles, imagining a gun-slinger tossing it into the air and shooting it down from the sky with a single shot from his colt .45.

As the summer months went by, Jack took a keener interest in the workings of the simple farm, studying production of the eggs that he now spent much of his time cleaning. This was far from a slick operation and, even at his young age, Jack considered he could streamline it if given the chance, by increasing the number of laying hens and reigning in some of the feed costs. The same could be said for the cattle, which seemed permanently hungry, grazing that pasture into the ground. He noted that old man Jarvis's evaluation of his cattle as "just somewhere for worms to live" wasn't far wrong. In his head, he made plans to increase output, which he would present to the old man one day, perhaps in return for a share of the extra profit, or even a partnership?

It was nearly a year later that Jarvis summoned Jack to him one evening via a message from a gal called Nora who kept house, a presentable young dark-skinned girl with a tempting smile and narrow green eyes. Jack had sat alongside her one summer evening as the fire flies skipped and danced across the orchard. Nervous initially but then compliant with the idea of maybe 'taking a walk.' The following day Rooster, one of the hired hands, noted the spring in Jack's step and made a point of pestering him about 'taking a walk' with Nora. It seems she'd done a lot of walking of late.

'I don't know what it's about, Jack,' Nora protested, scurrying behind him through the flock of chickens on the dusty yard as he strode towards the main house. This was only the second time old man Jarvis had called him to the house. The first was when he'd heard Sam Dogado had nearly removed Jack's head from his shoulders, more from the point of view of having an unexplained death on the property than much worry about Jack's well being. This time, Jack hoped he might be able to talk to Mr Jarvis about some plans for expansion. When he rounded the corner, seeing his boss pacing up and down on the porch, a newspaper in his hand, something told Jack that this might not be the right time.

Jarvis impatiently addressed the boy, thrusting the paper towards him. 'This you, son?'

Ready to deny everything, Jack glanced at the paper, folded open on Walter Winchell's gossip page of the New York Mirror and a highlighted headline. Of all the papers to choose and the places to put it, it was so like his mother to pick the society scandal pages to appeal for news of Jack. Winchell of all people too: that Vaudeville clown of a reporter, feared and courted in equal measure by the rich and famous and now relishing pitching into the hunt for the young Brooklyn run away through his column. It wasn't a great likeness, but it was unmistakably his grainy photograph with his name underneath it beside the words 'run-away from home and still missing'. Jack's heart sank. He was outed and he soon realised lying wouldn't help him.

'It say's you're fifteen, boy?'

'Not any more, Mr Jarvis, I had a birthday a few weeks ago.'

'I trusted you, Jack,' the man went on.

Jack squared up to him, nothing to lose now. 'And I said I wouldn't let you down. And I haven't. I worked hard for my pay; as hard as any older man!' This time Jarvis wasn't listening, his mind already made up and Jack had no intention of pleading.

'Too late, son.' His eyes rose to the farm road and a cloud of dust following a police car towards them. 'I'm sorry!'

## Brooklyn, New York - 1951

After a year away in the real world, school in Brooklyn had a different appeal to Jack when he re-entered the next term, clean shaven and well-washed. A year of hard graft had bolstered up his muscles too, to the point where, although not very tall, he had a healthy physique to match his over eager mind. An invitation to join the football team at first came as a surprise and he instantly declined the offer. However, watching the other lads through an upstairs window, strutting their stuff on the pitch and generally getting laid, Jack reconsidered. Within a week, he had signed for the team, taking the role of full-back from where he had chance to watch proceedings and assess the situation. Very soon he grew fond of the sport, despite the physical contact. In his younger school days Jack's surname had always been a target for those wanting to tease and bully and it was something he had gotten used to. But now, with some strong shoulders brought about by shearing sheep, he had learned to stand up for himself. In fact, he had become almost proud of the name Dick, which started to be revered around the school halls.

As well as football, the 8th-grade presented a chance to take on a few more responsibilities in the library as well as finding a trade in confectionary to some of the younger boys at a reasonable profit. Buckling down to his work, most of which he found easy, his grades improved and he found himself nearing the top of the class. In fact, within a couple of terms, Jack was named as the 'The boy most likely to succeed' in the annual yearbook, although this accolade could be attributed to the fact that he was the editor of the yearbook itself!

In October 1951 life was to change for Jack R Dick. Under persuasion from his family and paid for by his father, Sam, the now 18-year old set up home on the University Hill campus of Syracuse University along with another five thousand or so students, enrolled on a course in business studies. Having already set his sights on achieving better things, the university course to Jack was just a means to an end rather than an education. With a shrewd eye for deals, it wasn't long before he put up his hand for the post of Class Treasurer, something which would give him some hands-on experience in accounting as well as airing ideas and leading others on money-making schemes to maintain the balance of finance within his year. It was not only a job he relished but, unlike, say, sheep-shearing, he was good at. And with each money making idea that he explored and persuaded the others to go along with, Jack always made sure there was a little left over for himself.

Although Jack R Dick's family had been of reasonable means, he soon realised they were not even in the same league when compared to some of New York's over privileged elite, amongst whose company he now found himself. To some, the intimidation of power and wealth could be seen as a threat to ones social standing on a university campus but, to Jack – a young man who was learning to seek out opportunity from every situation – this chance to rub shoulders with some very rich kids was a mouth-watering challenge he couldn't wait to take on. Even at a young age, Jack was never one to rush into things without thinking through the detail and making, at the very least, an outline plan. As a younger boy, he recalled seeing the film of Robin Hood, redistributing money between the classes, while wearing a smile and some tight green pants. Dick smiled to himself now, as he, along with a few of his football-playing buddies, went about creating a tight card-school based in one of the rooms near the college. With some cleverly manufactured propaganda, the word got around that a night playing bridge along with some back-street Brooklyn boys could be quite lucrative. Stories of how these three or four guys continually lost money to those outsiders who were invited along to play. A few dummy players were enlisted, some of who didn't even know the rules, and sent on their way in profit to the tune of twenty bucks or so. One second-year student, Walter Perkins, whose father ran a dime-store in Arkansas, was so delighted that he actually won something, that he was ready extol the tale of his luck to everyone he met. Soon, Dick's little card school was being talked about all around the campus and, naturally, a queue of requests to join came flooding in via word of mouth. However, Dick was still not ready to snare his catch, while he and his chums compiled a list of likely candidates, wealthy enough to lose larger amounts without it declaring them poor. On the odd occasion, Dick would admit that he had got lucky, winning a few hands here and there and making enough profit so that they could keep the ruse going by sending away a few winners. The nightly card game had been running just three weeks when their first victim homed into view.

Lester Zowich was not a nice character, made all the more unpleasant - in Jack's eyes anyway – by the obscene way in which he flashed his money around, trying to impress. That is not to say it didn't strike a chord with some of the other students, particularly females, whom he wooed into bed with drinks and nights in high society establishments that most folks would never be allowed to set foot in. However, his respect for women was non-existent, using them at will and delighting in seeing them cry. Descendent of a long line of politicians and businessmen, Lester had had no use for respecting anyone, always getting what he wanted by flaunting the family name, right from his childhood. Having done his research, Jack considered that Zowich was probably waiting to inherit a large fortune from his grandfather while living on a weekly allowance that would have run the college funds for year. He was the ideal candidate to help Jack top up his own.

One warm Tuesday night, Lester Zowich turned up to accept an invitation to play, after Jack had turned him down a couple of times, feigning that they didn't have sufficient funds to play with the kind of money that went with Zowich's reputation. The room was set up with an emphasis on theatre gleaned from his mother's side of the family, where Jack would wear black clothes and a visor, smoking a fat cigar under a single overhead lamp. With the rest of the lights dimmed down, Lester could be forgiven into thinking he was in some ancient western film, as Jack nervously shuffled the cards and presided over the green beige table.

Even once the game was underway, Jack would still protest that he wasn't sure it was a good idea playing for such high stakes, letting Lester win the first three hands and be up by a couple of hundred bucks. But what the flash-man didn't know, and neither did Jack's own buddies, was just how smart he really was. Having been taught the game by his shrewd grandmother and then honed by playing his father from a young age, Jack's mathematical ability at bridge was about to be revealed. By the time Lester Zowich noticed that daylight was rising outside, he was out of pocket by over two thousand dollars. He was also out of humour.

As they shared out the money between them, once Lester had left the building in a half-drunken rage, Dick contented himself that a redress of wealth had just happened for the good of society. It has also been to the good of Jack R Dick, who had negotiated with his buddies prior to the event that he was to keep half the spoils.

Within a month, the set-up had been repeated at least five times, on each occasion the victim being one of abundant wealth and ignorance in equal measures. As his own personal prosperity increased, so Jack took to surrounding himself with the finer things that his money could buy. Exceptional French wine and brandy were bought through a chum whose father was in that industry, along with a few paintings and artefacts that turned his college room into a lavish reception where he would hold late night parties, inviting only those he felt would be of usefulness to forward his own social standing.

However, to Jack R Dick, his ability to win at mathematical games such as bridge was still neither exciting nor lucrative enough. Confiding in his friends that card games were still prone to runs of luck, both good and bad, his was a search for something more tangible from a business point of view.

With an ever increasingly impressive head for business, Jack was on the lookout for other opportunities. To start with, these came to him directly from the chemistry laboratory via a couple of pals enrolled on a science course. After the prohibition laws had been dropped in the nineteen thirties, the government had posed an unrealistically high tax on alcohol, something which, aided by the harder times of the second world war, had maintained the illegal sale of alcohol through the black market. By the mid fifties, with the country still reeling from the after-effects of the war, hard spirits often made their way onto the street via unofficial means. Before long, the vast chemistry labs in Syracuse University were losing stocks of pure alcohol from their stores which was unknowingly being diluted with pure water instead. Furthermore, a number of stills, which had been set up for experimentation purposes only, had been put to practical and professional nocturnal use, and gallons of freshly distilled neat alcohol found its way into clear bottles, which, eventually, found their way, through Jack R Dick, onto the street. To start with, dealing with some of the more hardened criminals who were leading the illegal trading of spirits around Syracruse was somewhat intimidating, even to a young man of Jack's confidence. Negotiations needed to be made, palms greased and risks taken, in order to maintain the supply chain. Slowly, but surely, Jack set up a line of receivers, learning whom he could trust, and which ones were outwith the law. It was a risky business, and one for which, despite his success, Jack found himself increasingly uncomfortable with. As well as the illegal spirits came some of the apparatus too, in the way of glassware, bell-jars and burners, all of which Jack also managed to dispose of at a handy profit.

During his spare time, he had picked up a copy of Dale Carnegie's *'How to make friends and influence people!'*, and read it from cover to cover at least three times. Quotes like 'Don't be afraid of enemies who attack you, but of friends who flatter you', made absolute sense to him. His personal favourite had been: 'Talk to somebody about themselves, and they will listen for hours!' To Jack, making friends was the easy bit. It was knowing who to make friends with that took a little more effort, but a challenge he was relishing with his whole heart.

By the end of his second term 'Jack the Peddler', as he had come to be known, had already gained a reputation as a man who could not only move pretty much anything that came his way, but one who had a reliable list of contacts in all walks of life. Indeed, Jack positioned himself as someone who was just as happy in the company of those with no money or prospects as he was with men of abundant wealth and means. This was not strictly true, but the skill enabled him to mix with anyone he believed could be of help to him, particularly when it came to making money for himself. It was through this list of contacts that he met a man, who had close associations with the military by the name of Laurence Hallford, an ex-lieutenant with an exaggerated limp and an ego to match. A wiry character with a pencil moustache, Larry had been through the war, based in mainland Europe and, along with his unit, been left pretty much to their own devices when it came to battle manoeuvres. It was during this time, while awaiting command, that Larry had used his wits to gather up 'things' that the war effort left behind, such as ammunition, French cigarettes and wine, a few pieces of antique china and silverware, as well as a German tank that had been captured, which went under the name of Elsie! For over a year, Elsie had been concealed from other units by storing her in a disused church under a giant sheet 'in case we needed the Lords blessing to help us fight our way out!' Although Elsie never made it back to USA at the end of the war, a number of Larry's other 'findings' did and soon found their way onto the market. With help from a military supply depot at the nearby Samson's Airforce Base, Larry soon discovered that it was not only overseas goods that could be traded on the civilian market, but US military supplies too. As well as his dealings in small arms and weaponry, Larry built up his own supplies of military clothing, household goods, furniture, bedding and a huge range of other products that, although second hand, could be marketed into civilian street.

A 'chance' meeting between Jack R Dick and Larry Hallford in a bar in downtown Syracuse had been nothing of the sort. Jack had read about Larry and his supply chain in a newspaper and made it his business to track him down. At first, the two men were cautious of each other but, as the drink flowed, Jack's charm seeped through, gathering Larry's admiration. As the conversation progressed into sales, business and the black market, so Jack put forward a solution to Larry that he was a man who could help him. At first Larry guffawed with laughter. 'What use can a young whipper-snapper like you be to a seasoned veteran?' Larry proffered. It was then that Jack unveiled his latest plan, based on a new idea that was sweeping the nation: that of mail-order sales.

Shortly they agreed that since Larry had access to all sorts of useful household objects, and Jack had a flourishing mail-order business, they could work together. The latter, of course, was complete fabrication, but wrapping up his beliefs of how the future would be into a tale of here-and-now was something that Jack was becoming adept at. By the time the two of them had drunk their way through a bottle of bourbon, Jack had enlisted himself as Larry's marketing arm to the retail sector. In a word, as his reputation on university campus had already labelled him, if Larry could supply it, Jack could peddle it.

The next morning, when he relayed his plans to his two closest pals, they looked at him in disbelief! Unperturbed, using the university library's facilities, Jack had drawn up a small leaflet, outlining a list of products, none of which he had in his possession, for sale. The leaflet was then reproduced by use of a copying machine in the administration building, operated by a pretty girl by the name of Suzie, with whom Jack had been more than acquainted over the previous months. By that evening, distribution of the leaflet had already begun amongst the student campus, with Jack making a phone call to Larry, and putting forward his first order of six dozen full sets of china dinner service, complete with cutlery and wine glasses. The price was fixed at $1.50 per set. Fortunately, Larry had not been privy to the leaflet, which advertised the sets and 10 dollars each, or nearly double that if they were purchased as separate items.

After the phone call, Jack made his way back to the card-school, to once more top up his income, confident that his latest efforts would soon bear fruit. That night, as though lady luck was taking a ride on his shoulder, he won over a hundred dollars from two young men he had never met before.

## Bayonne, New Jersey - 1955

By the time Jack R Dick left Syracuse University, he had not only paid for his course, lived in a lap of luxury, but was also in profit to the sum of an astonishing 15,000 dollars. Despite their differences, Jack's father couldn't help but be impressed, not only by his son's academic record but also his sense of business.

Sam Dick had started in the kitchenware business soon after the end of the war, setting up a small factory in Bayonne, New Jersey. In a post-war economy, where new homes were being built at a dramatic rate, the National Vanity Company soon started to flourish, finding outlets for their goods throughout New York and beyond.

'What do you say, Jack?' Jack and his father had retired to the sitting room of their surburban home, after enjoying a meal of meat-loaf. Jack's mother, Betty, was not the greatest of cooks but meat-loaf wasn't that difficult. They left her and Jack's younger brother, Elliott, in the kitchen clearing the dishes. The older man poured a scotch for them both. 'Time I took on a salesman, eh?'

Jack studied his father's larger frame. He was a grafter, that was for sure, spending far more hours at work than he should do. That was how America became great, especially after some duller years since the end of the war; men rolling up their sleeves and getting on with hard work, doing whatever it takes to succeed. And he had been successful too, building the company up year on year, often delivering goods himself and helping with installs. Sure Bayonne was a cheaper neighbourhood to live in than Central New York, but it was easily accessible into Manhattan, and the air was cleaner. His mother had complained at first when they moved out of the city but she soon fell into the ways of this suburb, seeking out friends whom she believed had social class. At least with a husband in the business, she could furnish the house in style, with new kitchen gadgets and a big pink fridge that was the envy of her friends. It was no place for Jack though, not somewhere a youngster would want to grow up amongst middle-aged mediocrity.

'A salesman?' Jack raised an eyebrow. 'Dad, you need more than a salesman. Look at you. You're running yourself into the ground.'

His father pulled himself upright, sucking in his rounding belly. 'Plenty years left in me yet!'

'You need a manager, Dad. That business has so much more potential, but you gotta delegate.'

Sam looked at his son, in his sharp clothes and bright eyes. 'A manager?'

'Did I say manager?' Jack pulled a big grin. 'What I meant was a managing partner!' Before his Dad could protest, Jack switched gears into his sales patter. 'Look Dad, the real-estate market is all about the younger generation now. America is changing and Eisenhower is trying to rebuild this nation from the ground up. Give the young ones a chance and let them lead the way. Build new homes and get them started. You need a route to that market. Someone those kids can relate to.' His Dad was nodding, so he continued. 'I got those skills Dad. I can sell that dream.'


Over the next year, Jack set up office in the New Jersey depot and started hitting the phones. Within a few months sales were up and soon he employed a couple more salesmen to get out there, knocking on doors. The family-based catalogue full of black and white pictures of empty kitchens was replaced with a brand new shiny colour one, showing curvy young twenty-something women, enjoying themselves, serving perfect meals to their young handsome men. Instead of a few pictures of plain white sterile bathrooms, Jack had a firm shoot photos of a blonde model with pouting lips in a tub full of bubbles, raising her leg while she sponged it down. That picture went straight on to the front cover of the booklet. In this game, the wife might get to chose the dream, but it was the man who had to pay for it, so you had to raise their pulses.

However, it wasn't long before his more risky marketing strategy was being questioned, especially by his mother who thought it highly disgusting to associate nude women with the family's high quality product. Jack had reasoned that the girl might be nude but nothing was on show. It cut no ice; Betty's friends had been talking. To Jack, that was a good thing: people talking was free publicity. He knew she might sniff at the idea but he also knew those same friends would admire the new car his Dad just bought, and the way the house had just been redecorated with the extra profits they were making.

No it wasn't her that was the problem. His father, a prominent member of the Bayonne golf club, also had his reservations about Jack's hard-selling tactics. A reference to the fact that one of 'his' salesmen had knocked on the door of one of the more affluent members of the club, pushing his foot inside while pitching in about deluxe bathroom suites, had gotten the old man into an embarrassing situation. That sort of thing was taboo around the more elite homes in Bayonne.

Soon the two started having rows and the old man was quite a formidable force in an argument. He was also none too keen on the way Jack spent money, all the time re-investing in new ways to promote and hard sell. The accounts often showed that Jack was ordering new lines of stock in such volumes that the bank account was unable to cover the cost until the products had sold again.

'You're going too fast, Jack!' Sam towered over Jack's desk. 'Too fast, and too far!'

For the next year, the two regularly come close to blows as business kept on improving. By Spring they had expanded out of their single block factory, buying up the place next door to store more stock. Jack had actually wanted to move the whole show to Manhattan, so they could mix amongst the real money, but his father had refused to sign the lease.

Eventually, Jack sat down and thought through a plan. Most of the work in the company was being done by himself, as he put in the hours, toiling over paperwork at an almost electric pace. His father was spending more time on the golf course, somewhere he said he could get time to think.

'Say, Dad.' Jack stood from his desk, keeping his voice calm. 'Why don't you retire?'

'What, at my age?' his Dad shook his head.

''Sure,' Jack continued. 'You could get a place down south, in the sun. Mom would like that. Play all the golf you want. This company is earning enough money to keep you.' He let the idea sit in the air for a second or two. 'Mom would soon get some new friends and,' he grinned, 'think of all those honeys on the beach...eh?'

With control of the whole business, Jack soon started to push the boundaries, taking more risks as well as spending more money on himself. He was once again back in an apartment in Manhattan, commuting back into Bayonne each day. To him, this seemed wrong, going against the traffic like that when everyone else was heading into town where the action was. He had promoted one of the salesmen to sit in as manager now he was the full boss and started to delegate some of the workload to him. With more free time and money on his hands, Jack expanded his social circle, joining a private club downtown and mixing amongst folks of influence. A late night session with one of his old college chums ended in him agreeing to put some company money into a stock scheme they were looking at. Next day, Jack pulled open the financial pages to find they had not only made a profit but near doubled their input. From then on, Jack took more and more interest in the share market and less in the bathroom business.

For the first time in five years, in 1958, the National Vanity Company started to show a dramatic decrease in profits. Sales were down, partly due to a slow-down in the economy but mainly due to Jack's lack of input and enthusiasm. It wasn't that he was bored with the business, more that he knew he could earn considerably more money on the stock market, especially if he gambled.

After a few heated phone calls with his father, he decided to fold the furniture company, pulling out what available cash that was left in stock and cash. Paying his father out half, he let the old man pick up the pieces while he shifted his attention into the higher flying deals on Wall Street.

With a personal float of 25,000 dollars, Jack then used incredible insight, gambling his way up the financial ladder. To an outsider, the unbelievable rising valuation of his portfolio on the New York stock exchange looked like sheer luck as he continually traded relatively unknown stocks at extensive profit. But, to those who knew Dick more intimately - and they were few - the certainty that luck had absolutely nothing to do with his rising fortune could not be more apparent. Although he would admit that he had an uncanny knack of identifying small companies that were destined to succeed in the future (the aim of any stock market trader), what set Jack R Dick apart from the others were his astounding sales techniques. Where most traders were schooled in mathematics, Jack was schooled in understanding people and then subtly persuading them to see his point of view. And he was damn good at it. Once he identified a company and labeled it as the next big riser, he would instantly be on the phone to his contacts in the press, the investment market and even his friends. 'This is a real winner, you can't lose...' These words were always accompanied by a winning smile.

And, in most cases, they *couldn't* lose, as folks scrambled to buy stocks in a firm that was going places. What they failed to know is that Jack had bought a high number of stocks on a lick and a promise, exercising his right to return them within a four day cooling off period if they did not rise. In short, the stocks he would trade were never even his to sell, not legally until he had paid for them. Furthermore, having announced his investment to fellow traders with a whisper that he had seen a preview of their 'shortly to be announced' accounts, and that 'these boys will have a big story to tell the world any day now'. Jack had, not for the last time in his life, found a loophole in the law and one that allowed him to get rich, very quickly. Obviously a rapid rise in fortune, even if it was only on paper, required a high level of borrowed money but that had never bothered him either. With a convincing enough story, there was always someone who would stump up the cash - this was something Jack was learning on a weekly basis. OK, once you started borrowing from outwith the banking system, the interest percentage went up and some of the lenders had fairly heavy handed ways in which to 'cover' their investment but, generally, the more disreputable the source, the greedier the lender. So if the return looked good enough, some of New York's wealthier lenders were prepared to take the 'gamble' on this hotshot youngster.

Within a year his personal stocks were worth a paper fortune of over 12 million dollars, one of the fastest rises in wealth ever recorded in the industry. But with everything invested in company shares, Jack was aware he was as vulnerable to the market forces as he was to the lenders underpinning his portfolio. A man always prepared to change tack if he saw a better opportunity, it was time to re-invest some of the 'paper' money into real assets. Having made it his stock-in-trade to seek out smaller companies with potential, Jack pin-pointed stocks in the Carpenter Steel Company in Reading, Pennsylvania, a business built on a more solid foundation than his own little operation. With a share issue due on the market to fund the company's growth, he had learned that a controlling interest in Carpenter could be bought for 1.5 million dollars. Started by James H Carpenter in 1889, this established business had pioneered methods of producing speciality steels such as stainless and alloy. With markets into aviation and the growing motor manufacturing business, Carpenter were poised to expand into Europe over the coming decade and Jack had full faith in their abilities to go global. All he needed to do was to gather a group of investors together and underpin a finance loan and he would not only be a paper millionaire but a bonefide businessman once more in a controlling position in the cutting edge marketplace. And, by now, Jack was getting pretty good at persuading people to back his judgement

However, not everyone took the view that this high flyer was always firing in a straight line and, to some, the dramatic rise of Jack R Dick's fortune was unquestioningly questionable.

One morning, in 1959, Jack was lying in the bath in his duplex penthouse apartment in downtown Manhattan reading the Financial Times with one hand and sipping coffee from a bone china cup with the other. A short knock came on the door.

'There are some gentlemen here to see you, Sir,' said his butler quietly, through the keyhole.

Towelling himself dry, Jack pulled on a blue silk

dressing gown, smoothing back his hair and checking himself in the mirror before opening the door. Roberts, a tall slender man dressed in immaculate uniform who had been his attaché for three months was waiting in the hallway outside. By the look on his face, Jack guessed that his visitors were possibly not just here for morning coffee. 'Should I invite them in, Sir?' As with seasoned butlers the world over, Roberts was not one to show any expression. Jack just nodded. While getting dressed, he listened to the curt conversation coming from the sitting room downstairs, as one man announced that the two of them were from The Securities and Exchange Commission and demanded to see Mr Jack R Dick immediately. Jack made sure he took a full ten minutes before nonchalantly wandering down the wooden staircase, dressed in a blue pin striped suit with red silk tie held in place with a gold tie-pin. On his way down he ran his finger over the gilt frame of his latest picture, an oil portrait of a field full of cows grazing in the moonlight.

'Gentlemen,' he addressed them from the third step, taking in the features of the two men, one having the appearance of an ex-con while the other was most definitely an accountant. 'How can I help you?'

The younger smarter man spoke first, pronouncing his words clearly and slowly. 'Mr Dick, do you know who we are?'

Dick made a point of sniffing the air. 'Well, I'm guessing you're not here to ready the gas-meter?'

The man reached into the inside pocket of his jacket, while the uglier of the two fixed Jack with a stare – one that implied 'you wanna run for it, sonny? Go ahead'. Jack ignored him, instead focussing on the bundle of sheets that his pal was spreading out on the table.

'My name is Johnson, I am from the Securities Commission.' He made no attempt to reach out for a handshake. Aligning the papers in order, he spread his slim manicured hands over the creases before looking up to Jack. 'Do you know what these are?' He beckoned to Jack to take a look but Dick's sharp eyes had already established what they were, in fact he had a pretty good idea what they were as soon as Johnson had produced them from his jacket.

'No?' he replied, dismissively. 'Are they my grocery bills?' Turning on a cheeky grin he turned to his butler. 'Roberts, are we behind with the grocery check?' Roberts made no attempt to answer.

'These,' continued the accountant, 'are copies of all your trading transactions for the last six months. Every transaction amount, beneficiary and date.' He looked up from the figures for a second. 'They make very interesting reading, don't they Mister Dick?'

'If you like sucking on my successful tailpipe?'

The man ignored the insult, pushing his glasses down his nose and peering closely at one particular paper copy. 'This one here, for instance?'

Instead of taking a look, Jack wandered over to the window, taking in the view of Manhattan. 'You can go on looking, Mister Johnson.' His voice was almost a sneer. 'You can look everywhere you want. I have a licence to trade stocks and that is what I do. Just because I am luckier than all the others doesn't say I ain't done it right.' He stopped, considering his words while wiping a speck of dust from the window pane. Then he spoke again, this time much slower and more pointed. 'Just because my deals are always good deals, doesn't give you a reason to go sniffing round my ass for gas leaks.' Jack turned to the little man and then glanced at his sidekick who had still said nothing. 'Is that how you get your kicks, Johnson. You and your pet monkey sticking your nose into places where…' He tailed off, turning back to the view again before adding: 'If you have something to say, say it. Or get the hell out of my apartment!'

Silence filled the air like stale smoke. Dick had forced the man's hand, just like he had done in all those poker games. He had been expecting the securities commission to visit any time now, but they wouldn't tell him what they had on him. Just a warning, that's all. Sure he had traded some stock he didn't own, who didn't? And maybe he had heard a few tip-offs - that was how the game played. Except that Jack R Dick just played with bigger stakes. Twelve million of them, to be precise.

'Do you know what kiting is, Mister Dick?' Johnson was holding his nerve.

'Sure. Did it all the time on the beach in Connecticut,' Jack's answer came back so fast that it was almost a believable statement. All the time he was thinking the game through. Stay one step ahead, Jack. Find out what they want and then sell them the answer. He smiled. 'Great fun when you're a kid. Not done it in a while though..'

'Ah, but you have Mister Dick. You have.' The accountant folded his glasses, looking directly at Jack. 'I have been watching you very closely, Mister Dick. You have made a lot of money.'

'Thank you!' Jack's tone was a little too facetious but all the while he was studying his opponent, seeking out the bluff. The man was good too. Good – or genuine.

'You have made a lot of money, illegally!'

So there it was: a legal accusation. Not a threat, just a warning. The man had a pair of nines, if that. Jack knew they would pick up on his little ploy sooner or later, purely by the magnitude of the figures involved. You didn't make 12 million dollars in one year without someone noticing. Sure, he had bought stocks he couldn't pay for, and underpinned his borrowing by moving checks from one bank to another. But he hadn't scammed anyone. Hadn't even taken from the rich as he used to at University. He had simply moved a few funds around, created a few days void in the system and then used the money to buy stocks cheap and sell for a profit. They might call it '*kiting*' but he simply called it business. And whatever else he may not be, Jack R Dick was good at business. He ran his hands through his hair, still staring out across the Hudson.

Before he had chance to challenge the man, he had produced another piece of paper from his pocket and laid it out on the table. 'Do you know who Edward Carter is, Mister Dick?'

Jack's heart skipped a beat when he heard the name. 'Erm, sounds familiar? Should I?'

'Yes, you should, Mister Dick. Because he is in your employ.'

'So what? I employ lots of people. What of it?'

'Do your employees buy shares on your behalf, Mister Dick?' Johnson's face was stern now, rolling out this accusation.

Jack considered this for a while, saying nothing, so Johnson continued.

'Did he buy these stocks, Mister Dick? Or did you buy them on his behalf? Under his name, as it were?'

Again Jack said nothing. They hadn't talked to Carter, he could tell that. And anyway, Carter wasn't one to turn him in. No, still Johnson had nothing on him that would stick.

'Did you, Mister Dick? You bought stock under one of your employees names?'

Jack still had his back to the two men and eventually he pierced the silence without turning around, with just two words. 'Prove it!'

## Downtown Manhattan - 1959

They would prove it, of course. Despite Jack's proclaimed innocence, his accounts were scrutinised right down to every cent. Dates were recorded and double-checked. A diary of deceit, the commission called it, as they uncovered movements of money through at least a dozen different banks, by check and wire, until the actual value became so tangled that only a genius could decipher it. Although Jack still believed that they wouldn't be able to piece enough together to convict him of anything fraudulent, what he hadn't banked on was the suspension of his trading licence, along with the freeze of all his assets, while they spent months on the conundrum. Although he had some of New York's brightest lawyers at his disposal, they couldn't get to work until a case had been made, and the longer that went on, the more Jack suffered. And therein was the problem.

With his trading suspended, he was no longer in the game of moving money around, and hence, the people whose money he had been shuffling with now started to demand it back. Within days of the news getting out about the SEC sniffing around Jack's paper trail, the deal buying Carpenter Steel soon fell from the table. And that was the one that would have converted his fortune into something solid enough that he could have traded his way out of. Maybe it was just bad timing, or maybe the SEC had wind of that deal too and struck out before he had chance to seal it. Now, with a pile of paper stock and a long list of creditors, the law suits came piling in and, even with some of the best lawyers on Wall Street, there was no way to halt the changing tide. Still declaring his innocence and, in some cases, counter-suing the lenders themselves for disreputable lending, what money he did have in assets rapidly got eaten up by the lawyers.

Not only had the Carpenter deal gone west, but the group of investors he had already signed up were none too happy either. A couple of them had made quick deals, selling stocks to gain the cash they needed and some of that had already got eaten up in preparing arrangements for the deal ahead. Their outrage didn't help Jack's cause any, as words of his falibilty started to ripple around the market traders. Lawsuits quickly piled up.

For a while he relished the battle, taking on the big boys and enjoying fighting their fire with his own. Jack R Dick was a winner, always a winner; a man who could stand up to them! Someone who could win over hearts and minds with his charm, something that had never let him down.

It was only a matter of months before he realised that perhaps the fight wasn't going his way and soon, his resonance started to weaken.

At first it would be just the odd moment of doubt; a quick shimmer of uncertainty racing through his veins before he shook it off with a flick of the wrist. But, as each day grew longer, so the gloom manifested itself until it lasted for hours – and then days. Here he was, the great man, a man so brimming with self esteem that he could talk God himself out of a few bucks, now reduced to 'the accused!' With no income, he was resigned to 'letting Roberts go,' and then shortly afterwards, with a couple of month's arrears, the apartment too.

He had met the girl Kerry a few months earlier in a bar in Greenwich Village. Born near Cork in Ireland, like so many students of the time she had travelled to New York unsure of what she would discover there. Although younger than him, Jack found her intelligence refreshing and her laugh infectious. In fact, couple that with her long dark hair falling in ringlets over her shoulders and legs that seemed to go on forever, he soon became infatuated with this beauty. Always one to tease, Kerry found Jack's charm quite amusing, suggesting that that smile would get him into trouble one day. It certainly got him into her bed.

As the months went on, with his mind more preoccupied with making, or in this recent case, losing money, she had drifted on and holed up with a tall Dutch man with long blonde hair and an Afghan coat that smelled of chemicals. Jack wasn't exactly jealous, and admitted that her amorous manner was far more suited to someone of that nature, resigning himself to the fact he could have hung on to her, had he so wished.

'Hey,' Kerry smiled, her eyes glistening. 'How you been?'

Where normally Jack would chirp up that things had never been better and that today was the next best day in his life after yesterday, somehow he felt he couldn't lie to this girl, as though she could see into his soul. Anyway, it was him who had called her up and asked to meet. 'Oh, you know,' he replied. 'I had better weeks.'

'Jack, down on his luck,' she wrapped her arms around him in a hug and he could feel her warm breath as she spoke softly in her Irish brogue. 'Surely not?'

He shrugged, forcing a smile that she could see straight through. 'You got a spare room I could use, for a few days?'

Over the next few weeks, his home was on the couch of a stranger's apartment. By night the place was one constant party, with loud music which wasn't entirely to Jack's taste, and the comings and goings of folk who barely knew each other, just turning up on a whim, usually carrying a few vinyl records. The place smelled permanently of cannabis and incense, again neither of which were of Jack's persuasion. However, by day the apartment was quiet as most of them slept through till early afternoon. Jack had no idea what these guys did for money, but they didn't seem to have a job between them.

Each morning he would rise and shave, sometimes before the last revelers had even gone to bed. A quick coffee and he would be out of the door, heading down to his Wall Street lawyers, a world away from the one he had just left.

Occasionally he would get chance to have long serious conversations with Kerry in the early evening, when they both would sit out on the fire escape, her telling tales of rolling green fields back home in Ireland and how it rained all the time and everyone was poor. More than once he mentioned the time when he had run away from home and spent a summer cleaning eggs and shearing sheep. The great outdoors, he said, was where his future lay. Kerry would laugh, of course, she always laughed, but then she would sit and listen silently as he thought his plans through out loud, convincing her and himself that farming was the future.

One evening a knock came on the door, a gruff voice asking if Jack Dick was home. Sending Kerry to field the visitor, he again made use of the fire-escape, taking off his leather shoes so that his feet couldn't be heard on its metal tread as he made his escape. With more creditors chasing him, Jack would head downtown to the safety of his lawyers by day. On some days, when he couldn't even afford the cab fare, he would walk the whole five miles, , all the time trying to fight off the demons in his head that were bringing him down. He consoled himself with the fact that Manhattan was far too noisy anyway, for a boy who had 'farm blood' in his veins. On his way home, he would stop in a bar and sit and drink bourbon until his speech slurred. Sometimes he got animated with anger about the markets, and the system in general.

'There's no room in this lousy country for the little

guy,' he would regale. 'Where is the free enterprise that made this land great, huh? No sooner you climb up, they wanna shoot you down.' Most of his buddies concurred, although perhaps they too despaired of the speed which Jack had climbed the financial ladder, leaving some clever minds in his wake. 'We should all go and be farmers!' Jack continued. 'Plant a few seeds, keep a few cows, then sit around and watch the calves and crops grow while you spend the summer fishing.' When it was pointed out to him that pretty much every farmer in the land worked from daylight till dusk the whole year through, Jack wasn't listening. In fact, he so wasn't listening that he was already planning an escape from the city into the countryside. It had always been a dream and it still was. All he needed to do was rise above this current crisis and then take his life in a new direction.

It was a damp Tuesday morning when he woke to find a note sitting next to the kettle in the meagre kitchen with his name on it. On it, in beautiful swirling hand-writing, Kerry explained that things hadn't worked out with her and Jan and she had decided to move on West. She wished him all the best in whatever he decided to do and the last line just said, 'I believe in you, Farmer Jack!'

Jack folded it into his coat pocket and at that moment he knew his bad days were over.

Yes, his company might be bankrupt, but Jack had other personal assets. He had always been a collector: coins, jade, silver, ivory, coral, porcelain, china, first editions, rare book bindings and antique English furniture were all amongst his prized possessions and now he would have to finance himself out of this mess. After giving the matter some thought on one of his early morning walks, he decided that it would be the postage stamps that would have to be sacrificed. Like everything Jack involved himself in, he had become rather an expert in stamps, something that had always fascinated him.

When he was a child, his grandfather had collected stamps from the mid eighteen hundreds and, after showing a keen interest, had given the collection to his grandson in his will. From there it had been a boyhood obsession, but unlike other boys of his age, who collected stamps of the day, he sought out Penny Black's and Blue's. These had been the very first stamps, created in middle England in 1845, and some could be bought in local markets for as little as a few dollars. Very quickly he established that it was not just the stamp that made the value, but where it had been posted. For instance a New York marked Penny Black might be worth five to ten dollars, whereas one that had been posted in, say, the Mediterranean island of Malta could be worth twenty times that amount. There were others too, which he soon learned to recognise from magazines, such as the Basel Dove, a rare Swiss three-coloured stamp that seemed to go up in value every month. He also learned to study the post marks in finer detail, practising them over and over with a soft pencil on transparent paper. It was surprising who could be fooled by an innocent looking child.

Together the small collection was worth something near one hundred thousand dollars.

## 21 Club, Manhattan - 1959

'I need some air,' he told a close pal over a few brandies. 'I have to get away from all these crooks and get me some space. Some room to breathe. A place to think!' All the time, his eyes looked beyond his colleague, distracted by a tall slim girl sitting on a bar stool sipping a martini. Her blonde hair hung down to her bare shoulders, shielding her face from view. Yet, from that first glimpse, Jack knew that when he saw it, it would be the most beautiful face in the world. Since Kerry had left he had found other girls, of course. In fact, if you mixed in the right circles among the rich and famous in New York, girls were never far away. If he had wanted to, he could have had a different girl every night like some of the guys did. Jack preferred them just one at a time.

Still keeping one eye on the vision, he turned back to his colleague, after he had stopped speaking. 'Yeah, yeah. I hear ya. I'm not cut out for hard graft, is that what you say?' The man nodded.

'And farms cost money, Jack,' his pal continued.

'You real-estate guys are all the same.' Jack sniffed. 'Always hung up about the price of things. They might have some of my cash on ice, but I still got means, Tommy. I still got means. One phone call, and I could have a loan in no time. Buy myself a little place out in the sticks. A few cows out in the meadow and a horse to round them up. Gotta be better that running amid this bunch of losers!' Jack swung his hand around for effect, as he emphasised the word 'losers'. With whisky now flowing through his veins, he was about to stand up and make his 'little man' speech when his eyes flicked past the girl at the bar to another man further along.

'Say, isn't that Bing Crosby over there?'

Before Tommy could turn around and get a better look, Jack was already on his feet and heading across the bar. Tommy rolled his eyes and watched him go. He had seen it all before. One minute he and Jack would be talking business, or politics, or some other engrossing subject when Jack would spot someone he thought to be more important, and simply wander off, leaving a deal or conversation in mid-point.

Crosby was amongst a group of men, all immaculately dressed and engaged in conversation. Now back to his usual confident self, Dick tapped one of them on the shoulder and then, as he turned around, he slipped in behind him, holding his hand out to the singing film-star. 'Mr Crosby,' Jack said loudly. 'I would like to personally welcome you to Manhattan.' The statement was accompanied by a smile.

Tommy watched the situation unfold from a distance before signaling to a waiter and then whispering in his ear.

Bing wasn't so loud in his reply, but cautious nonetheless. 'That's very kind of you, Mister....'

'Dick. Jack R Dick. It's a pleasure to shake your hand, Sir.' Jack signalled to the bar-tender. 'Now please let me buy you a drink?' Before Bing has chance to decline, Jack had instructed the man, 'same again, Dodds.'

A little taken aback, Bing eyed Jack for a second before nodding his head. 'Well, thank you Jack. But there really is no need. I can just about afford my own you know.' This rallied a loud laugh from his colleagues, all of whom had been awaiting his retort, and now turned their eyes to Jack to see his reaction.

Jack never missed a beat. 'Well, if that's the case, Mister Crosby, you'd better buy me one!' With that he swooped down the bar, putting his arm around the beautiful girl sitting on the stool. 'And one for my girlfriend, too!'

To begin with, Bing's friends went into a deathly hush, hearing this upstart present himself in such a way and focussing their master's expression. Within a couple of silent seconds, Crosby's face creased into a smile. 'Why of course, dear chap.' He looked towards the pretty girl, turning on his best smile. 'Please do introduce us, Jack!'

This was a game, and both men knew it. Here was one of the world's finest actors with possibly the most recognisable singing voice on the planet, challenging a young cocky upstart to a duel. And at this present moment, the score was one-all but the advantage definitely in the famous man's favour. Again, Jack never missed a beat, instead putting his arm around the girl and pulling her tightly to him. 'This, Mister Crosby, is one the finest actresses this side of the Blue Ridge mountains. Take a look at this face, Sir. Because next time you see it, it will be on a huge screen.' Both men took a look at that face, one which should have been reeling with embarrassment, and yet was remarkably calm. Jack let silence fill the air one more time, hoping his little ploy had worked. It was a gamble, but then that was Jack R Dick's middle name. For the first time he realised it wasn't just himself that was being silent, but just about every other male in the bar, each one watching the scene play out. At last the girl's eyes stared into Jack's, a smile erupting across her face. Still she said nothing. Eventually Jack broke the stalemate. 'Well, dear. Aren't you going to tell Mister Crosby your name?' He could feel his own heart pounding, as his whole reputation hung in the balance of a total stranger. Again he pulled her tight to him and this time she responded by uncrossing her legs and stepping down from the bar stool, the long curves of her tight satin dress exposing themselves for the first time. You could have heard a snowflake fall, as every male eye in the place explored her physique. Still silence.

Crosby broke first. 'Well, my dear. Cat got your tongue?'

'Lynda,' her smile widened further and Jack thought it was the loveliest smile he had ever seen. 'Lynda Terker, pleased to meet you. Jack never told me he mixed in such select company.' She held out a hand which Bing took and kissed in a most theatrical way after which she turned back to Jack, her smile fading slightly. 'Why didn't you tell me that, Jack? What with us practically engaged to be married and all.' Lynda's voice was a smooth as the silkiness of her long dress. 'You are always full of surprises, aren't you?' Her eyes were boring into him now.

'Mister Crosby just offered to buy you a drink, Lynda.' Jack knew there was no backing out now, as he put his arms around her once more, placing a kiss on her cheek. It was warm to the touch.

'Scotch!' she purred, 'on the rocks, thank you!' With that she sat back on the stool, crossing her legs once more. Jack stood awkwardly beside her as Bing was about to advance towards her, to check out this young thing who has aspirations to be an actress. Before he took a step, a bell-boy marched up to him from behind, tapping him on the shoulder. Bing turned around to address the young man who was holding a card in front of him.

'Telephone call for you, Mister Crosby. On the desk in the lobby, Sir.' The boy was virtually trembling as he made his address. 'Said it was urgent, Sir!' Bing turned back to Lynda and then to Jack, recognising the faint relief in Jack's face.

'If you'll excuse me,' he turned back to follow the bell-boy and then stopped and spoke back over his shoulder. 'If we don't meet again, good luck with that wedding!'

Once he was out of earshot, Lynda whispered in Jack's ear. 'Well, Jack. That was some stunt you pulled. Is this how you get all your girls?' Just by the warmth of her breath and the sweet smell of her perfume mingled with a faint tint of whisky, Jack was convinced this was no ordinary girl.

Putting his own lips close to her ear he said, 'Only the ones I really want to marry!'

## Downtown Manhattan - 1960

Nervous breakdown is not an exact condition, more a state of mind – that is what people told him. His own doctor had said that it was up to him to alter his state and see the sunnier side of life. But it wasn't that easy – anyone who had been there could tell you that. Despite what they said, it wasn't just a case of smile and the whole world smiles too, cry and you cry alone. It was more the knowing that inside you is a genius awaiting its next chance, while all around is oppression which inspires depression. The inability to get out there and make a deal had festered until he was almost a recluse in his own home. Even the girl, Lynda, who he loved deeply and shared his inner-most secrets with failed to fully understand what it was that was holding Jack back. When he exposed his wish of being a farmer, she stood by him in principle, although failed to follow his passion. On the darker days, Jack would cast his mind back to those few cows on a small farm in Connecticut, and how he had hatched a plan to make the little business more successful.

One day while at his lawyer's office, his faithful old attorney sat him down and looked him squarely in the face. 'For God's sake, Jack. What are you going to do with yourself?' These few words were the final catalyst he required to spur him into action.

'I am going to become a Gentleman farmer!'

The reply met with exasperation. 'Jack, you are a bankrupt stock trader, who has wound up just about every financier in New York State. Are you out of your mind?'

Jack would have replied that to the contrary, he was considering a plan. At first it seemed impractical, almost ludicrous, but the more he mulled it over, he believed in his own convictions. He chose to say nothing more to the older man.

It had been an article in the New York Times that had upped his interest in cattle, explaining how the cattle business in Scotland had been booming since the war. The narrator had said that, if you wished to be seen as a successful entrepreneur in Britain, during the forties and fifties, you would have bought a small farm and stocked it with prize shorthorn cattle, a breed that went back hundreds of years. As the fifties gave way to the more affluent sixties, it was the black Aberdeen Angus cattle that were more in favour. A few examples were quoted, where a wealthy textile magnate had sold bulls for upwards of ten thousand each while another property tycoon was also running a herd of cows in the south of the country that were equalling these figures.

Over the last few years, Jack's dream had always been to run a farm breeding horses. In fact, he had often picked up the Racing Post, glancing through the breeders and particular stallions that had made their mark on the industry. But what made one particular breeder successful? Was it down to luck? Jack doubted that very much. No, like any other subject, these men were experts in their own field. A pun indeed, a farmer being outstanding in his field. Jack chuckled to himself over that one.

He had discussed an idea at length from his friend Tommy, who had been dealing quite successfully in real estate, and who had tried to persuade Jack to join him in that career. The scheme was quite simple, where a group of buyers would all invest in a property portfolio, each paying in large sums of money, often buying up property off-plan from builders who had not even put a spade in the ground. With a rising market during the late fifties, some of these investments had proved very lucrative for some, often doubling their money on stocks within a year or two. But, to Jack, the gains weren't high enough to interest him on a small scale, particularly if you took into account the high tax rate that was applied to capital gains on property. Jack had given it some serious thought but just couldn't see himself in that market.

The more he considered it though, the more the principle worked the same for livestock. And the difference was, farmers didn't pay tax. Well, not at the same rate that the richer folks paid it. That was what the article had said, that wealthy British businessmen were buying into cattle as a tax loss. Well it hadn't used those words, but it had definitely insinuated that a loophole in the law allowed them to buy farms and bloodstock, and then sell the produce at agricultural tax rates. What was it they had called it? A tax shelter!

'That's it. Cattle real-estate!' He jumped up from his chair, pacing the room again, like the business man he had always been. This was another chance. A chance to combine his love of the farm with his love of business!

Tommy looked at him quizzically. 'Did you say CATTLE real-estate, Jack?' he asked slowly. As usual, Jack wasn't listening, instead his mind was whirring at a hundred miles an hour.

Up until now, he had labelled small-time cattle breeding as a 'Ma' and 'Pa' operation, just a way of whiling away life without putting in too much effort. But, according to the figures he had read, the price of beef might be cheap enough, but the price of breeding stock was a hundred times higher. With absolutely no knowledge of the cattle breeding industry, Jack went out and bought a copy of Farm Week and started thumbing through the pages, particularly reading up on anything to do with cattle and beef production. Near the back page he saw an advert for courses in agriculture.

'I will go back to college,' he announced to Lynda.

'College? You never learned anything the last time you went there?' She smiled at him. 'I thought you were a man who learned on the move. Self-taught. That's what you told me.' Holding his hand, she looked into his eyes. 'Jack, why don't you go into real-estate with Tommy. He seems to be doing well. You would be great at it, with your sales skills? In fact everyone seems to be making money that way just now, Jack.'

'That's it. Don't you see? Too many folks already chasing the same market. Everyone cutting prices and commissions to compete. What it needs is something new, a new phenomenon, something low risk, high reward – and tax free! And most of all, something fun!'

'And you are going to college to find a new market?'

'No, I, Lynda, am going to learn to be a farmer!'

Lynda gave him a look of pity, her head on one side, as if to say 'Really?' She would have spoken but he put his arms around her.

'And you, Lynda Terker are going to be a farmer's wife!

## Cornell College, Ithaca, New York - 1961

Within a few weeks of enrolling in Cornell, Jack soon realised that farming was no different to any other form of business. You bought some stock, mated it or planted it, and then reaped the rewards. But what he had in mind for his future in the business was a little more complicated than that. While other students, mostly half his age and possibly with half his intellect, took notes from a mumbling lecturer about gross margins and capital outlay, Jack had already scouted through the library and was studying animal breeding. A number of books about animal husbandry offered quite comprehensive details about feeding and raising cows, and the rotation of pastures and cereals, but it was a small leather bound copy of a book called 'Inbreeding and Out-breeding' by professors East and Jones that really sparked his imagination. Written some fifty years earlier, the book dealt mainly with the study of genetic make-up of grasses and cereals, although some of the later chapters applied the same principles to animals, including Man. Words like out-cross, hybrid-vigour and recessive genes were explained in detail to those with an intense interest bordering on the obsessed. Jack found it fascinating, to the point where he sought out other information on the subject, lapping up knowledge of how the gene pool actually worked in principle.

From there, his attention turned back to the Aberdeen Angus breed, which was rapidly becoming as famous in America as it had been in its native country of Scotland. A few phone calls managed to get him copies of a twice annual booklet produced in Scotland, featuring breeders and prices from recent sales. Jack studied these in intense detail, memorising bulls and breeder's names and following their progress through each publication. It appeared that, despite there being over a thousand bulls at the annual sale in Perth, it was just a few men who dominated the scene, where names such as Haymount, Eastfield & Newhouse usually featured among the highest prices. The annual studbook listed every animal registered with the Aberdeen Angus Cattle Society, a hierarchy of well-to-do men who oversaw the business from an office in Aberdeen. Jack studied recent copies in finite detail. Also he managed to purchase a history book about the breed, charting its progress from a few black cows in the north of the country, pioneered by just a few great men such as William McCombie and Sir George McPherson-Grant who experimented with breeding until they arrived with the great black breed of cattle towards the end of the previous century. Jack read it, and re-read it, watching the rise and fall of certain individual breeders who had come and gone over the years. One thing that tended to characterise these great men was that they were all entrepreneurs, not unlike himself.

Likewise, the Association of Angus in North America also supplied him with information, where forward thinking cattlemen were turning to the breed, selecting seed stock from Scotland and shipping them across the Atlantic. It seemed that the main contributors to the high prices of the time were the Argentineans, many of whom were regularly paying upwards of 20,000 dollars for bulls, most of which were no more than 10-12 months old. The cattle business in South America had been boosted by the demand for corned-beef and the Angus was highly suited to its production, with smaller faster growing animals providing the right kind of beef for its manufacture. More recently, a few names from North America had started to feature, some of which included quite well known families of senators, business magnates and other notables who were dabbling in pedigree cattle. Jack took a particular interest in one herd which seemed to be dominating the sales in Chicago, that of the Leachman cattle company. It was time to pay them a visit.

## Chicago stockyards - September 1961

The first thing you noticed about the Chicago stockyard was the smell. In a city that got its nickname from the inclement weather, the stench from a compound of 10,000 head of cattle would carry on the breeze for a couple of miles. Build in the 1870s on swampland in the south of the city acquired by three railroad companies, some 2,700 wooden pens stretched out as far as the eye could see and each one was packed tight with animals awaiting their fate. The Dinner of America: that was what they had branded this place.

Jack looked across the pens from the high platform of the train station, studying the animals, mainly black Angus or Herefords with their mucky white faces. This was the business end of the deal, and not a place for the faint hearted. People loved to see cows grazing, swishing their tails in the wind on lowland plains. And they loved to eat beef too. It was just this part in the middle that was kept away from the public persona.

It was a good experience to see the lines of cattle and the meat packing plants beyond, dismissing hides and effluent out the back door whilst sending out prime beef through the front. This area was known as 'Bubbles', from the way the swamp absorbed all the mess, churning it through its swampland and then bubbling back to the surface. It wasn't just the land that was rough either, being located in one of the windy city's worst neighbourhoods. Let's face it, anyone who earned their living in this industry would be hardened to its appalling sights and smells to the point where nothing would worry them too much. Down a side street, the notorious O'Leary's Bar and Grill, started and run by Jim O'Leary, one of the hardest

Irish immigrants in the area, was now a watering hole for cattlemen who earned their living riding the railroad cars, herding the cattle into town. But it was beyond O'Leary's and the squalid streets that held Jack's interest. Towering behind the yard, the great exhibition hall stood like a sentinel; a piece of magnificent architecture rising from mist of sweat and steam below it. He had seen pictures of the building, inside and out, but nothing prepared you for the first real sighting and its surrounding squalor.

Dressed in a fine tweed suit he had borrowed from a friend, beneath a heavy mohair coat and equally heavy brogue shoes, he stepped down from the platform and weaved his way in the direction of the hall. It wasn't an easy passage as a variety of folks shoved and pushed, all heading in the same direction. All the talk on the train journey had been that of Angus cattle. Jack had listened intently, taking in two or three conversations at once, while all the time his mind worked through a plan. One young man was going to work as a cattleman for Senator Ryall, one of the better known breeders of the time. This was his first trip to Chicago and it was obvious he was extremely excited. Another, more well-to-do couple were visiting the show because the lady's brother had some exhibits entered in the National competition. One thing was for certain, Angus cattle certainly stirred the emotions of many.

At some point in the throng one man had spoken to Jack, interrupting a conversation he had been listening to at least three rows away about how the price of breeding stock was on the increase. Jack had to ask the man to repeat the question.

'What was that, sorry?'

'I was just asking what was your involvement at the event, Mister?'

Jack broke off listening to the distant couple, in favour

of the man nearby, considering his thoughts. On this reconnaissance trip it had been his intention to gather as much information as he could, while remaining fairly anonymous. For two weeks he had been conjouring up a plan and now he had to be sure it was feasible before he let it out of the bag.

'Oh, I am just here to invest in a few cattle,' he proffered. 'I heard that Angus cattle make a great investment. I am thinking of putting in some capital.' Jack gauged the man's reaction, and that of the few people around him in the carriage. Soon a few of the other conversations came to a temporary halt.

The man responded favourably. 'Well, Mister....?'

'Dick. Jack R Dick, New York.'

'Well, Mister Dick, you are talking to the right man. Tomson. Clint Tomson.' Jack shook his outstretched hand. 'And I just happen to be a cattle buyer!'

Jack made a mental note of the name, checking out the man in his sports suit and Stetson hat who was delving in his pocket. He pulled out a card which Jack took from him and glanced at it for a second before putting it in his top pocket. 'Thanks, Clint. I'll bear that in mind.'

After that, Jack made an excuse of needing the toilet and left the conversation. He didn't want to get too involved just now, but the man could be a handy contact for later. He was also quite delighted at the prospect that his announcement of investment into Angus had caught the instant attention of a number of enthusiasts. Shortly the train had come to a halt and Jack had stepped out on to the crowded platform.

As the exhibition hall loomed nearer, the enormous size of it almost took your breath away. Inside, more rows of cattle took up a large part of the floor space. But these weren't cattle like the ones out in the stockyard, waiting to be slaughtered. No, these animals were much more refined, with silky back hair all groomed into place, lying in clean fresh straw. Unlike the ones outside, these Angus cattle all seemed happy, sitting in rows tied up by the neck, all chewing their cud. Young stockmen bustled about, up and down the lines, one man grooming away frantically at his charge. Jack glanced up at the signs hanging over the animals, denoting which herds they were from. He stopped and looked at the beast for a minute, eyeing up its rotund shape, rounded belly and square rump. In his mind he was comparing it to those ones he had seen in magazines and papers, training his eye to look at the real deal. The young man looked up at him and gave a half smile.

'You like my steer, Mister?' There was a sense of desperation in his voice, as though it was imperative that he got a positive vote from every passer-by.

Jack nodded without speaking, letting the nervous young man continue.

'Just fourteen months of age, and weights eight hundred twenty pounds.' He glanced up to a piece of paper pinned on a wooden rail above the animal's head, which confirmed the weight and age. 'A whole twenty pounds heavier than anything else in his section.' The paper also gave information of the parentage of the beast but, Jack noted, there was no ribbon to show it had won a prize in the exhibition. As if reading his mind, the boy confirmed that. 'He's out in the next class.'

Hurriedly the young chap untied the halter of the animal and started to lead him up the alleyway towards the show ring, gathering in confidence. Jack spoke to him for the first time. 'Say fella, do you know where I would find Mister Leachman?'

The man stopped dead, and looked back. The uneasiness was back, as he studied Jack again, perhaps realising that he may be more than just another tourist at the event. 'You know the Leachman family?' It was the way he said it that took Jack by surprise, as though he was asking to see the president

'Sure I do,' bluffed Jack. 'We go way back.'

The boy's mouth dropped open for a second, before pointing in a vague direction of the other side of the hall. Next time he spoke it was almost in a stutter. 'Over there, top corner of the barn, nearest the sale ring. Always has the same pens every year.'

Jack nodded his gratitude and watched the boy resume his passage towards the show ring, as others appeared from their stalls and followed along in a line. As he neared the corner of the barn, a number of men were fussing around one small black animal, overlooked by a large framed man who dwarfed the beast. Smoke puffed out from a cigar in Leachman's mouth, billowing out from under his heavy Stetson hat like a hedgerow fire.

Born in Adamsville, Ohio, to James and Alice Leachman, Lelend (Lee) and Lester (Les) were the youngest of seven brothers. Lee, seven years the elder made his mother proud by being the first from the family to attend Ohio State University, where he majored in livestock, spending much of his time in the stock barns and gaining a reputation amongst his peers as a keen cattle showman. Learning from leading geneticists such as Dr Carl Gay about breeding and selection, his education was topped up by master herdsman JB McCorkle, a man of Scottish descent.

After he graduated he landed the role of riding the boxcar for the El Jon herd in Iowa, a job which gave him invaluable experience as they scooped up trophies around the state fairs in 1939. When the herd was sold, young Lee went along with the package.

Meanwhile, his younger brother Les had also worked his way through the same course at Ohio, also featuring as an enthusiastic basketball player. Again shining as a prominent and talented cattleman, along with his friend, Herman Purdy – who went on to be professor at the University before achieving global fame in the cattle business - his college course was cut short when he was enlisted into the army for National Service. It would be three years later before he could complete his graduation, in 1947, now married to Ruth. During his earlier college years, Les had been persuaded to work alongside his bother in Virginia, fitting out cattle for the International show.

Both with sound bovine grounding it was inevitable that one day these two able boys would start and run a herd together. To begin with, it was a wealthy magnate and chairman of the Royal Typewriter Company, by the name of Senator Alan Ryall, who bankrolled their first venture into cattle breeding. Between these men, the name of the Ankony herd would not only be created but cement its name into the history books for the next sixty years, during which time it would change owners a number of times. Not afraid to splash out big money to grab the headlines, in 1959 Lee Leachman stood his ground at the formidable Perth Bull Sales in Scotland, fighting off Southern American and British breeders to secure the young bull Elevate of Eastfield for a then world record price of 25,000 guineas, the equivalent of 40,000 US dollars. It was Lee's old boss, McCorkle who was under-bidder. Owned in a partnership with Aberan Farms, the bull rapidly became a breeding phenomenon in both herds. By the early sixties, the Chicago International Show had become their own playground as Ankony racked up win after win, picking off not only the Grand Champion title but most of the others awards as well on a near annual basis. It was widely recognised that although Ryall was the money pit, it was Leachman who was the brains of the outfit where he was held in near celebrity status amongst other breeders throughout the nation and beyond.

Jack had done his homework on Leachman, singling him out as a man who had as much a midas touch in the cattle world as he himself had in the world of general business and sales. If his plan was to come together, then this would be the man who would help it succeed on a large scale.

Dick waited his chance and then strode up to the big man, holding out his hand. 'Leeland Leachman? Jack R Dick. It's an honour to meet you, Sir.'

Lee looked down at the smaller man in his trilby hat, then down at the outstretched hand, before taking it and near crushing it in a powerful squeeze.

'You buyin, or sellin?'

'Oh, I am definitely sellin, and you are going to do the buying, Lee!' Jack's smile almost caught the man off guard but he steadied himself, picking up Jack's gaze. Jack completed the silence as the two men locked eyes. 'I have a proposition that I reckon you would be interested in. What say we meet at O'Leary's, eight o'clock tonight?'

Leachman let go of Jack's hand, still holding his gaze. 'Make it eight tomorrow morning. Might be busy celebratin tonight.' Jack nodded compliance as the man turned his giant frame away.

'You better not be wasting my time, Dick!' he called back over his shoulder, but Jack had already diverted his attention back to studying the cattle being paraded around the grand ring, as if ignoring the man now he had his appointment. In fact it wasn't just the cattle that he watched but the faces of the onlookers themselves. All his life he had a knack of sniffing out wealth and here it was at its most opulent. People with an abundance of money tend to adorn themselves with the most splendid clothing, as though trying to impress. Here was a mixture of the best silk woven suits and Scottish tweed that was only available in the top designer outlets at extortionate prices. Jack studied a couple watching the bulls with intensity, him in an ill-fitting expensive hat that was a size too small and her in a flowing white coat and blue silk scarf and designer boots that looked like they hurt her feet. They were both looking up at the animals and then checking details in their printed catalogue, analysing parentage, growth weight and any other crumb they could find to improve their knowledge of the cattle world, so they could purchase some breeding stock and impress their friends. Jack took his mind back to Leachman for a second. That man had forgotten more on a Sunday morning than these phonies would ever learn. All Leachman had to do was win some prizes and they would be putty in his hands, selling them middle-class cattle at top-class prices. Sure, Ankony had some of the best animals in the hall but they also had some pretty mediocre ones as well, and those were the ones lined up for these suckers, come sale time. Just like when Jack had been selling furniture, share stocks or anything else that had come his way, he was convinced that with a little more knowledge than they had, he could easily sell them a few Angus breeding animals. In fact it wasn't just the animals they would buy, it was the dream that went with them. For a while he studied that crowd, as the wannabe winners clamoured around the real winners, those with the ribbons on, as though even being near these prized animals might transfer some of their magic. It was pretty obvious that each and every one of these visitors shared that dream, the one where it was their own animal winning that Grand Champion prize. Maybe, one day, it would be them being interviewed by Johnny Carson on global TV. He almost sneered at the overdressed couple now queuing to touch the first prize bull as though they might learn something from it. One thing Jack was convinced of, that these pair would never gain the knowledge to produce an animal like this in a hundred years, not without someone else's help. And that is exactly where Jack Dick would fit in.

O'Learys was a daunting place for the uninvited visitor. Due to the nature of the cattle business in these parts, it rarely closed through the night, as cattle arrived at the stockyards around the clock and their handlers needed food and alcohol. During International week, the whole place intensified as pedigree breeders mingled with local hands, some of whom held a different opinion of what the purpose of a beef animal was. To slaughtermen, cowboys and dealers, it was all about the beef, beef and nothing but the beef. Sure a bull needed to be able to walk a few miles out on the plains but, ultimately, it was just a machine to furnish the dinner plates of a nation. To some of the older guard, the fancy ways in which the few hundred bulls in the exhibition hall were pampered and groomed was alien to them, and the exorbitant prices also. Discussions on the subject would often turn into fights, especially as the drink flowed plentifully. The combination of Irish origins and Irish whiskey would regularly degenerate into mass brawls where bare knuckles would knock lumps out of each other, bodies spilling out into the street like something from a John Wayne film. There had been some legendary fights over the years, with tales retold through generations, many of which featured the boss himself. Jim O'Leary, a huge short-tempered horse of a man from west of Ireland, had been known as king of the stockyards back at the turn of the century. As an immigrant during the growing times of the meat industry in the area, Jim had provided accommodation for thousands of his fellow Irish workers, as well as drink and gambling.

The needs of Irish cattlemen, any cattlemen for that matter, required a third ingredient to make up their day and night, and that was women. Sure there were a few cowgirls but they weren't the sort of females that a man would want to snuggle up with after a long day - to the contrary, those sort of women were more likely to bite off your ear and steal your wallet than whisper sweet nothings to you while you investigated them. The whores in and around the Chicago stockyards were nearly as legendary as the cattlemen themselves. In the earlier years, women with long flowing dresses, overly adorned with makeup, would parade out front like prize animals themselves. By the time the fifties came along, the business had become a little more low key, although it was still pretty evident that anyone of the female persuasion who hung around at O'Learys and didn't smell of cowshit was probably available for the right amount of dollars!

The hotel rooms had been rough, and the bar rougher. Although the men worked in squalid conditions and earned very low wages, most of what little money they did have found its way into O'Leary's cash till, by one route or other. His reputation as the King had not only stemmed from his business dealings but from his prowess as a street fighter, and a man who stood no nonsense in his establishment. In his earlier years O'Leary had kept some quite interesting company, at a time when Chicago was not a place for the faint-hearted. Running a bar through those times of prohibition required the help and collaboration of some of the most powerful men who controlled the city, men who had the police force in their pocket. Years later it was his association with bad company that eventually got him killed.

Jack studied the photographs on the wall in the near empty bar, bowing his head to take in the details of hundreds of men working together in terrible conditions, afraid to complain as there was an endless queue of immigrants to take their place. The bar was quiet this time of morning and, amid the stench of stale beer and cigarette smoke, he considered the stinking mephitis that those men would have to endure while dealing with all the rancid offal that was a by-product of the 'great' meat business. It was no wonder that they eventually formed into Unions, so they could demand better rights. O'Leary had been the go-between when the unions called men to strike, taking money from both sides like a true businessman and Jack Dick admired him for that. Yes, a lot of men had made their money in the cattle business, but the real winners were those who could take a little piece of each of those men.

A loud shout came from a room at the back of the bar which turned Jack's head in time to see a man dressed in denim and a Stetson hat leaving via the side door, cursing over his shoulder. A few other men were shouting after him, jeering him almost. It was a situation that Jack had seen many times before, especially in his university days. These men had probably been playing poker all night until one of them got cleaned out, probably losing his week's wages. He glanced at his watch, 7.45am, as he sauntered over and looked in through the open door.

Just three men sat at the table now, the one in the centre leaning back in his chair, hat pushed back on his head to reveal a wide smile that supported a short cigar in one corner. 'Wondered when you would show up,' he bellowed.

Jack took in the small smoke-filled room, the sort of place he recognized; his sort of place. He had never had Leachman as a gambler but then all men were gamblers really, in one way or another, especially the successful ones. Without saying a word, Jack pulled out the empty seat and sat at the card table, the two other men eyeing him as he did so. By the look of their eyes it was fairly obvious they had been here all night, although Leachman looked fresher, scrubbed and shaved, as though he had had a good night's sleep.

'Five card stud, that's what these ruffians play around here!' The man was already dealing, all the while looking directly at Jack, cigar smoke curling under the brim of his hat. The pile of notes in the centre of the table looked fresh too, as though just pulled out of a wallet rather than been gambled back and forth for hours. Again this was familiar territory to Jack Dick, a man who had bankrolled himself through college by setting up poker games.

'Sure,' was all he added to the conversation. He knew how this would go, the big man was scouting him out, getting to know a bit about him and how he operated. Well the same could be done in reverse. You learn a lot about someone from a poker game, especially if you want to do business with them. One of the other men dealt him two cards which he left face-down on the table for at least a couple of minutes.

'I heard about you, Dick. Done some pretty good deals.' Leachman turned over two cards. 'And some pretty poor ones too?' Jack's eyes never flinched as he quietly studied his cards, letting Leachman continue the conversation. 'So what makes you think I got time to listen to anything you say?' Still Jack remained silent, awaiting his chance. 'Want to buy a few cows, do ya?' Leachman shook his head. 'Nah, word on the street is you ain't got a dime. Maybe you want me to loan you a few cows, Dick?' This sparked a chuckle from the other two men. 'You gonna play that hand or not?'

'I'll raise you a thousand,' Jack's first words since he sat down. This time his eyes narrowed as he stared at Leachman. 'And another hundred grand if you come and work for me!'

# PART II

## Wappingers Falls, New York State - 1961

'Wow, it's beautiful, Jack. Can we afford this?'

Jack wasn't listening to his wife, as he studied the house from the outside, admiring the intricate ornate woodwork of the vast white porch. They knew how to build things, back then, not like the rubbish that his pal Tommy was touting. He glanced up to the apex roof above the porch, one lone shuttered window peering out on the second floor with views across the plains, above a stretch of five more huge windows drawing the sunshine into the first level. This was proper real-estate. Inside the house was even more splendid, with high ceilings and crystal glass chandeliers flooding the hallway in tiny flecks of colour on the parquet floor. Jack was already imagining his large framed paintings on the stark white walls, sporting prints of cows and horses grazing in fields. This was a gentleman's house and he would be that gentleman, oh yes.

His wife was speaking to him again, tugging at his sleeve. 'Jack! Can we afford this place?'

Still keeping his silence, Jack wandered outside towards the barn. This was the business end, where he would make his mark on the world. Not only could he house his cattle in this expanse of a building, but he could showcase them too.

Lynda joined him at the doorway and he spoke to her for the first time since they had gotten out of the car. 'This,' he said, theatrically waving his arm toward the empty building. 'This is how we can afford it. One day this barn will be home to some of the finest bloodstock in America.' She followed him as he walked towards the paddocks, three or four square ones of about an acre each, all surrounded with wooden railed fencing. 'This will be the showpiece. Famous animals will graze here; the sires of champions.'

'But the money, Jack. What about the money?'

'I got it covered. I did a deal.' Jack was used to keeping things from Lynda and she knew it. It had been a long hard decision but one he had come to terms with, to sell his vintage stamp collection. Eventually he had put the whole lot up through an auction house and it had made a decent price. Admittedly he had gotten some investors interested beforehand and had played one off against the other. A few telephone bids had come in anonymously as well, thanks to Tommy and a couple of other pals. The final figure of around two hundred thousand wasn't quite enough to finance this place, but Jack already had that business in hand too.

That first night he had seen her at the bar, Jack had already known who Lynda was. The Terker family were well known in upper circles of finance, most of them bankers. Jack had once met her brother, Richard, and it was back to him he went with his new idea. With some persuasion, Richard had stumped up $300,000 for a half share of the new venture.

'You did a deal, Jack? What sort of deal to get us into a place like this? Maybe we could rent it for a while but we surely can't own and live in a place like this, can we?' Lynda pulled on a cigarette glancing out across the flat grassland and beyond. 'What will we do with all this land? And who will help me in that house? I can't run a house this big, Jack...'

'Do you like it?' Jack gave her that smile, the one that she, and very few people could refuse.

'Like it? I love it!'

'Well, you better go and check out the rooms, because

the furniture arrives tomorrow.' He kissed his wife on the cheek, heading back towards the barn.

Wappingers Falls Ranch had belonged to Elliott Crosby, brother of Bing, who had kept a few cattle there, as well as some horses. The word that it was coming up for sale came through Tommy, who had a pretty good handle on most of the real-estate in New York State. It needed some work to fix up the cattle side of it again, but the horse paddocks were ideal. The farm came complete with Carrie and May, two maids who were sisters and would help Lynda in the house. There was also one old farmhand although Jack doubted he would have much idea on the sort of business that was going to be run on this place from now on.

Within a couple of days, a lorry with some furniture had arrived, some of it of their own and some from Lynda's parents who had far too much of it in their old house in Connecticut. The mixture of old and new had caused a bit of a discussion but for now it would have to do. Jack made sure his few antique chairs were positioned in the hall where they could be on show, as well as hanging his dozen or so paintings in the hallway and above the fire in the large dining room. He assured Lynda that soon they could replace all the other stuff with something more modern if she wished, once they had the business up and running.

It was Saturday morning when he asked Lynda to set the table for dinner that evening, as they had guests arriving. An hour later a pick-up truck drove slowly up the drive, its two inhabitants looking out at the creaky old barn and horse paddocks.

Jack welcomed them with a handshake. 'Leeland, Lester, glad you boys could make it?

'I thought you said you was in the cattle business, Dick?' Lee ducked his head out of the pickup and then stood to his full height. 'Don't look much like a cattle business to me. Looks more like a ghost of a place to me!'

It took Jack most of the morning to show the two men around the place, Jack confidently regaling them with facts about how he would build a coral here and fix up the barn into a showpiece. All the time he was taking on advice and listening to the two men talk to each other. By late afternoon, Lee was coming round to seeing that Jack at least done some research on breeding cattle.

'Well, you sure as hell don't look crazy but that has to be the most downright absurd idea I have ever heard. If you can sell that, I reckon you could sell a boat load of sand to the Mojave desert!'

'You just supply the cattle, boys,' Jack let out a laugh, 'and let me do the sellin!'

## Attorney's office, Manhattan - Jan 1962

Jack sat across the shiny table from his two lawyers. 'Well, don't just tell me what I can't say, tell me what I can!' He stroked his chin, thinking. 'Why is it you fellas always see the bad side of things? This is a goldmine, I'm telling ya.'

'Jack, you have nothing to sell. Just an idea, that's all,' the older attorney was doing his best to get Jack to see sense - something that was never easy to achieve. 'I have been with you for four years now and this is by far and away the craziest thing you have come up with. You really think you can persuade folks to buy something that doesn't exist. Look what happened last time Jack. Look what went wrong, for God's sake.'

'Aw Howard, this is different and you know it,' Jack's self confidence was almost infectious. 'The last one was just bad timing. If I had secured that steel company, we would have been home and dry.'

'Different? You can say that again, Jack. At least you were selling something that folks could relate to. Shares, real-estate, that's where wealthy folk put their money. Something with some security, Jack! Something with a track record!' He raised his eye to the ceiling. 'But cows? Bullshit, more like?!'

'I keep telling ya, it's not just a few cows, they are buying a part of a successful whole set-up. A money producing scheme that doesn't pay tax. They'll buy it, you see?'

The lawyer raised his voice. 'But the cows don't even exist, Jack. Just a few empty fields and a whole pile of debt. And your history in this town ain't exactly smelling of roses either. You're not even allowed to sign a check, remember?'

'That's where you come in. You need to set up the company, use references to some top cattle breeders like the Leachman boys and create a few trading figures. Make some up if you have to. I have decided to call it Black Watch Farms. Has a kind ring to it.' Both men were now protesting but Jack wasn't listening. 'We need a company secretary, then we need some marketing literature, photos of pretty cows suckling baby calves, a few blue ribbons, that sort of thing. Then pop in some forecasts of profits above, say 40%, and we get this show on the road.'

Jack stood to his feet, decision over, leaving the two bemused men looking at each other. 'Now Howard, you with me on this, or do I have to fire your ass and get some proper lawyers?' He ended the meeting as it had begun, with a wide smile, one that said, 'Trust me, this is a winner!'

## Wappingers Falls - March 1962

'That's what I like to hear. Thank you Dr Redman, you won't regret this.' Jack put down the receiver and looked up at the young couple sitting on two antique chairs across from his desk. 'Sorry Mister Douglas, where were we?' He shuffled a few papers and then glanced through a sheet of A4 in front of him. Lester says you got a lot of cattle experience, Garfield.' He continued reading before putting down the paper and looking the man over. 'But what I need is someone who can not only run a farm, but a multi-million dollar operation. You reckon you can do that?'

The thin young man sat upright in his chair, squeezing his wife's hand next to him. 'I sure do, Mister Dick. Been working Angus cattle all my life; ain't much I don't know about that side of it. I learned my trade from boy to man. Even ridden the boxcars. And I have run farms too, back in Virginia.' He turned to his wife. 'And Patti here, she's a good worker. She can help out in the offices or the house.' Patti smiled. 'Hell, even the kids can help out around the place if you want them to?'

As was getting more often the case, Jack wasn't listening, or didn't appear to be. Garfield Douglas decided to stay quiet and let him think, watching Jack's eyes as he looked blankly past him at the wall over his shoulder. Resisting the temptation to turn around and check was Jack was looking at, instead he studied a painting on the wall of some black cattle grazing on a low meadow by a river. An old black and white striped farmhouse and some buildings with straw rooves suggested that this was probably a scene in England rather than the US although the rolling landscape reminded him of back home in

Virginia.

'Constable!' Jack's voice pierced the silence like a pricked balloon. 'Painted some wonderful English landscapes. But they tell me nobody wants to look at cattle on their walls anymore. All about horses, these days, so they say.' Jack was fixing him with a grin this time. 'What do you think Garfield, cattle or horses?'

'Definitely cattle, Mister Dick.'

'Good! You start Monday. You can have the cottage at the end of the lane, should be big enough for you and,' he checked the paper in front of him before continuing, 'five children, is it?'

Garfield let out a smile. 'Yes sir, five great kids.' He stood up, displaying excellent manners by holding out his hand for Dick to shake. 'My friends call me Gar, Sir!'

Jack shook his hand. 'Well Gar, welcome to Black Watch Farms. You have got a busy time ahead of you. We need some more quality Angus cows here very soon or this lot will start yellin at me.' He waved his hand theatrically over the piles of paperwork on his desk.

'How many head of Angus do we have already?' Gar was asking.

'Precisely none at all, Gar. Not one! So we'd better get shopping!'

'And how many are we looking to buy?'

'Let's start with 200, eh?' He looked up at Gar who looked surprised. 'What, don't you think that is enough? No you're right. Let's make it 300! For the first six months, anyway, and see how it goes.'

Gar stared at the man. 'Let me get this straight. You want me to start Monday and buy 300 head of Angus females in the first six months?'

'Not just any Angus females, Gar. The best we can find. My clients only want the very best! You tell Leachman that! You work for me now, so you make sure those boys don't try and pull a fast one!' With the impatience in that statement, Jack had intimated that the interview was now over.

Patti was awaiting her chance. 'Sir, would it be okay if the kids brought their own horses? Only it's a long way to go visit them in Virginia?' She finished the question off with a bright smile.

Jack returned the smile threefold. 'Sure. We gonna need a few cow-boys and cow-girls to round up this lot. Are they good with horses?'

'Born and raised.'

'Good, well they can probably teach my two young ones how to ride.' He turned back to Gar. 'Anything else?'

Gar tried not to splutter at the enormity of the task he had just been given, as he collected his hat from the sideboard. 'I am gonna need some staff, Mister Dick. I can buy em cattle, but I sure can't look after that many head on my own.'

'Let's not get bogged down with the detail, Gar.' Jack was showing the pair of them to the door of his office. 'Just get this show on the road and you can choose your hired hands as you go. Bound to be plenty of experienced men on the farms you'll be visiting would relish the chance to work for Black Watch Farms. We pay top rates.'

Just as they were descending the stairs Jack called Gar back. 'Just one more thing,' the infamous smile was back, 'to save me travelling with you, you'll have access to the company check book.'

## Sotheby's Auction House, New York - June 1962

Brian Watson shifted uneasily in his chair as the man opposite questioned his every sentence.

'Cattle paintings might look very nice, especially with your farming connections, but it is horses that are in demand these days.' Watson spoke in a clear English voice, tinged with a New York slant. Even as a young man his knowledge of the art world, and eighteenth century prints in particular, was among the best in the city. It was fairly obvious that this was the reason he was being questioned by this new buyer on the block.

'You're telling me my cattle prints are worthless?' It wasn't exactly a question as a realisation, as Jack ran his hands through his slicked black hair, thinking.

'Sporting art, Mister Dick. British sporting art.' Brian laid a sale catalogue on the desk in front of him. 'This one was sold through our London auction house. We don't get to see many of them over here.'

Jack studied the picture in detail, running his fingers around the tail of a horse, while reading the inscription below. 'Diamond, by Ben Marshall.'

Watson let the silence fill the air as he encouraged his new client to get drawn into the painting on the page, watching the man's eyes study every detail like a true pro. Eventually he said 'Marshall of Newmarket is always in demand. This one was of particular interest to the market, as it was later engraved in mezzotint by William Barnard.'

'Looks like it,' said Jack, turning his face away for a moment. 'Fourteen thousand pounds is a lot of money.'

'Some say it was cheap,' Watson smiled for the first time. 'But what would I know?' The two men locked eyes as though a bond was forming. Both knew that each one would be useful to the other.

Jack eventually broke the stair, pushing back his chair to rise to his feet. Watson followed suit holding out his hand. 'Good to meet you Mister Dick.'

'Likewise, maybe I will be in touch.' Jack gave the hand a firm shake.

'One thing I will add, though, Jack. Do you mind if I call you Jack?' Dick shook his head. 'One thing, Jack. Those Brits.' He corrected himself. '*We* Brits, are not too keen on letting their prized paintings out of the country...'

## Wappinger Falls Ranch - May 1962

'He ain't much to look at, Jack. But he seems to be breeding well.' Gar listened as his boss answered on the other end of the phone, before speaking again. 'Yes, Sir. The bull is called Elavate of Eastfield. He was Perth champion, 1959, and bought for Aberan Farms for a record price of 23,000 English guineas.' Gar tipped his hat back on his head in the heat of the small office in Virginia where he was using the office telephone. An electric fan spun overhead, pushing the heat around but doing little else to cool the place. 'I dunno, Sir. In fact I'm not sure they want to sell him at all. Leachman reckons he is quite happy to keep him till he dies of old age, Sir.' Gar stopped again, wiping the sweat from his brow with a red handkerchief. 'Thirty thou..' He gasped and then lowered his voice as a girl behind the desk raised an eyebrow. 'Thirty thousand dollars, are you sure? He's a four year old bull, Jack. He ain't never worth that much.' Listening again. 'Well I know he was a record breaker in Scotland, and a Perth champion but that don't make him worth that much as an old bull!' He glared at the girl who looked away. 'OK Jack, you're the boss. I'll do what I can.'

It was three days later when a large semi-trailer cattle truck pulled up the drive to Wappingers Falls ranch livening up a cloud of brown dust as it did so. Jack saw it arrive from his office window which overlooked the drive, closed his ledger and put down his pen, and went to meet it. He wasn't the only one as half a dozen men were also scrambling to get a look at this latest purchase.

A day before the bull's arrival a press release had already gone out that a world-record price animal had been purchased by Black Watch Farms on behalf of a number of investors. The purchase price had been $60,000 and, according to head cattleman, Garfield Douglas, this price had been cheap compared to what this bull would be able to breed. The actual price had only been 20,000 but there was no need to tell the public that. What they didn't know wouldn't hurt them and Leachman wasn't going to tell. Besides, the more expensive the bull was, the higher they could value its offspring.

The wagon reversed up to a coral near to the barn and unloaded firstly 20 black heifers which, to Jack's untrained eye, looked just the sort of animals his investors would want to see. All shiny coats and rounded bellies, with big ears and short legs, they looked just like the ones he had seen in the magazines.

A special pen had been erected by one of the young cattle-hands who had turned out to be a dab hand at carpentry. Jack had arranged for a local sign-writer to stencil a plaque to go on the gate of the pen saying 'Elavate of Eastfield, 1959 Perth Champion and world-record priced bull.'

He, and a few of the other boys watching, had to admit that his first sighting of Elevate, he was a little disappointed. The bull was quite thin compared to the cows and didn't look much like a champion at all. Gar came to Jack's side as the bull settled into his new home, after being led out by one of the boys. 'It was your call, Jack,' he said quietly.

'As long as you think he will breed, Gar. But you are going to have to feed him up a lot. This is a showpiece. And we need to impress, you get that? Once the word gets around that we are spending big money, every man-jack in this state is going to want to have a look at what we got.'

'Understood, Jack. I'll have the boys give him a wash this afternoon. We can soon fatten him up. He has been running out for 50 head of cows for six months. He'll mend in no time.'

'You got three weeks, Gar. I'll hold em off till then, but he'd better be ready.' Jack was looking across at the 20 cattle spreading out in the paddock, their heads going down to graze immediately as they fanned out. 'And most of those heifers are in calf to him?'

'All of them.' Gar gestured. 'Some of them calving quite soon.'

Jack was already losing interest as he turned and headed back to his office. To him it was all about the show. Those heifers had costs 500 dollars each and he had already got some of them sold for five times that amount to a dentist and his wife from Milwaukie. Gar didn't need to know that. Not right now. But he would have to stall the buyer before he came to look at his purchases, maybe spin them a yarn about quarantine or something. Hopefully by the time they came across to view their investment, the bull would be in better condition and maybe some of the cows would have calved already. They had paid for them in advance, of course, enough money for the eight animals to pay for the entire shipment. And also, with a little persuasion, they had advanced 6 months worth of payments for the animals' feed and keep, plus their transport, a charge for their bull-service and a one-off cost for calving them. In fact, the couple were so delighted with the deal, once Jack suggested that sons of these animals by a world record priced sire would be worth tens of thousands that they couldn't thank him enough for letting them in on such a great deal. And it was a good deal. Looked after by our experts, the cows would maybe live to nine or ten years old, and have a calf every year, repaying their investment twenty to thirty fold.

That was Jack. A man who could offer a great deal: one too good to resist. All he needed was to seek out the money and then let him have five minutes to close the sale.

Such was the response to his new scheme that he had taken on a couple of salesmen he used to know in New York, to get out there amongst their wealthy clients. He had sat down with these two guys and explained the deal in detail, and both seemed sceptical at first, especially when he told them the whole thing was a 'gift' from the IRS. The scheme went like this.

While America was still trying to pay off its national debt since the war, anyone earning in excess of $200,000 per year would be paying 91% tax! Welcome to a new legitimate scheme, endorsed by the government: A Cattle Tax Shelter!

As a high income-tax payer, the client could legally invest money into certain non-profit making schemes to avoid tax. A $20,000 investment would buy four top quality pure-bred cows which would be farmed on their behalf by experts and with all expenses, such as feed, transport, handling etc being tax deductable. When the cow had a calf, if it was a bull, it would be sold on the clients behalf and they would reap the profit, after deducting more expenses, and pay tax on it at preferable agricultural rates. However, if the calf was a female, it would be added to the herd and the value of that client's investment would go up. After a minimum of three years, the client could withdraw their investment, valued at the 'going rate', but would only pay capital gains tax at 20% instead. Obviously, the longer they left their money in the scheme, the bigger the herd and the bigger the profit. But most of all, it would be fun.

Of course, there would be certain things the client didn't get to know, such as the initial cost of the animals, and the annual profit cuts that Black Watch would be taking, but that was the nature of business.

What he needed now were some 'high profile' investors and fortunately, due to the circles he moved in using his charm and influence, Jack had access to plenty.

## Perth, Scotland - February 1963

'Is this the calf, John? He's fair filled out since I saw him last.' The two men studied the animal in front of them, while a young man held the white rope halter, a constant grin on his face.'

'Aye,' replied the taller of the two, 'he has that.' John Rugg was an experienced cattleman who had been around the Aberdeen Angus breed for most of his life. A large man in a narrow brimmed hat, he leant on a long shepherd's crook, which supported his tall frame. He knew how the game went. If an animal was good enough there was no need to sing its praises, especially not to a potential buyer such as this one. Anyway, the man had been the judge this year and had already awarded the bull a first prize in the junior class of the show.

Now the stouter man studied the calf again, walking around the front of the animal. 'A bonny head, but maybe not good enough for my cows.' He tapped the young handler on the arm. 'What do you think, young man?'

'I think he is good enough for your cows and everyone else's, Mister Adam. Question is, are your Newhouse cows good enough for him?' the boy grinned.

'Now Charlie, that's enough of your cheek. Know your place, boy!' Charlie felt his boss's glare and his cheeks reddened.

'Sorry, Mister Rugg.'

Mister Adam returned his smile and studied the bull calf for a few more seconds. 'Evulse, you call him? Well, his mother was a good beast right enough. We'll maybe have a look at him later.'

The two men watched Bob Adam walk on down the line studying the rest of the cattle with equal interest. Adam, one of the most respected breeders in the cattle business, was a revered opponent, especially when it came to buying a stock bull. His Newhouse herd of cattle at Glamis Castle, maternal home of Queen Elizabeth, The Queen Mother, was one of the most famous names in the world, when over previous years he had had numerous champions at Perth and achieved top sale price and sale average more times that anyone else in the last decade.

'Do you think he will buy him, Mister Rugg?' Charlie, an athletic young man with a broad Orkney accent was hopping from foot to foot.

'I reckon there is a fair chance, boy. I reckon there's a chance.' John watched the boy tie the bull back up in its stall under the overhead gantry. 'Now you stay here and don't leave his side. There's room enough for a bed until morning by that bale there.'

'Yes Mister Rugg. You can trust me Sir.'

Up above was an overhead gantry where people were milling around, chatting away about this animal and that sire. Perth bull sales were the pinnacle of the cattle trade in Great Britain, particularly for the Angus breed. For nearly one hundred years the old market on Caledonian Road in Perth had been the mecca for breeders, coming to sell their hopeful young bulls, or to buy stock. Many good men dreamt of a win at Perth, where nearly 1000 bulls would be competed against each other, and, more often than not, hopes would be dashed and dreams destroyed. Young Charlie Gorn has been brought up on a farm on the Orkney Islands off the North Coast and had shown promise as a cattleman with a future. After a fortunate meeting with Bert Rugg, a young man of similar age, Charlie had been recommended for the job at Lindertis Estate where a relatively new herd had been set up by the owner, Sir Torquil Munroe, under the guidance of Bert's knowledgeable father, John. As a young apprentice, his job was to muck out the stables and comb and groom the young bulls four times per day, while he listened to tales from the older men about the great Perth sale. And now here he was, being left in charge of a first prized bull and one that may well be among the top prices. Over the last couple of months, he had dreamed of taking Lindertis Evulse out into the show ring and had been practicing leading the bull around the stockyard at home.

After making sure the animal had enough hay to keep him contented, Charlie shook up some straw beside the beast and lay back with his head against the railings, chewing a piece of straw himself. Overhead he marvelled at the old metal ornate pillars that the supported the roof of this institution. Built during the Victorian era, when craftsmenship was everything, the whole fabric of the place absorbed and exuded the excitement that took place during the first week in February every year.

He glanced back at the red rosette pinned to the barrier in front of his charge and then was just closing his eyes when he heard some louder voices approaching. Sitting up straight he spotted four men making their way down the alleyway, looking down at the bulls, most of which were now sleeping. At least three of the men in the throng wore unmistakable wide-brimmed Stetson hats and Charlie's heart skipped a beat.

Earlier in the day he had seen a few of these men and there had been whispers around the market that they were here to buy some of the best cattle. Jack jumped to his feet and encouraged his bull to stand up, rapidly brushing the straw from his back and sides and then quickly combing the animal's hair.

The thinner blonde-haired man of the bunch spoke first. 'What do you think about this one, Lester?'

'Not sure he'd be big enough to breed from.' Leachman

studied the calf for a while. 'Maybe got potential though, Gar.' He looked at Charlie. 'The boss around, boy?'

Before Charlie could find his tongue, the equally imposing figure of John Rugg hoved into view and nodded to the three men. 'Lester, Gentlemen.'

'John, this is Jack Dick and Gar Douglas, from Black Watch Farms. Think they might be interested in your young bull.'

Jack was the first to reach out and shake the man's hand. 'Jack R Dick, good to meet you John.' He flashed a smile that, to anyone who knew him, meant it was already time to make a deal.

'Bull's here for sale, same as all the others.' John looked unimpressed with this man in his sheepskin coat and trilby hat. 'You want him, you'll hae ta bid for him, just like the others.'

Jack stepped forward, pulling John Rugg out of earshot of the others. 'John. How much do you want for him? Because I am looking for an expensive bull. Do you hear what I am saying? You fancy making the headlines, John?' John was listening. 'We, that is, my investors and I, would like to buy your bull for perhaps a record price. We can make sure that happens, can't we John. You know how this works.' All John did was nod his head, so Dick continued. 'What is the current breed record, twenty nine thousand guineas?' Again, John nodded. 'So, John. You tell your bosses that, once the bidding exceeds that threshold, and your bull has just made a new breed record price, everything it makes above that is to be returned back to me. I will sort out the rest with the auctioneer. Understand?' Dick winked at the man. 'That way, everybody wins.' Once more John nodded his head, without saying a word.

Jack turned back to his entourage, who were joined by another man in a tweed suit. 'Ah, Clint. Good to see you. We may have a little job for you.'

Two hours later, Charlie Gorn led Lindertis Evulse proudly towards the crowded sale ring, pushing his way through a number of eager onlookers, all passing the opinions on this bull, that bull and the trade in general. Not too many of them gave this young bull a second glance. Just another bull, from an unknown breeder.

The sale ring was no bigger than ten feet across and surrounded by men sitting and standing; collectively a bunch of men with more knowledge of cattle breeding than the rest of the world put together. High up in a wooden rostrum, an auctioneer called Eddie Hutchinson banged his gavel down onto the desk. 'One hundred and ten pounds, final bid.' He pointed to a burly man in a beige smock: a well known butcher. 'Your bull, Sir.' The bull he was referring to left the ring by another exit and Charlie was signalled forward, his heart pounding.

'Right gentlemen. What do we have here? A first prize winner from Lindertis. Some good back-breeding in him. A good bit of growth, too. Come on now, get me started. Give me twa hundred pounds.' The crowd didn't seem to be taking much notice so he rattled his gavel a couple of times to demand their attention. 'Do I hear two hundred. And fifty. Three. Four, five. Five hundred I am bid. Five hundred, five.. six, eight, one thousand. Any advance on one thousand guineas?' Charlie caught sight of Bob Adam raising his little finger. 'One thousand I am bid,' Eddie shouted out as crowd still seemed to be ignoring this animal.

'Five thousand!' The voice came from behind the railings, as the crowd went instantly silent. '

Eddie looked across to the voice. 'Did you say five thousand, Sir?' Clint Tomson just nodded, as Eddie turned back towards Bob Adam who raised his finger again. Eddie gathered pace, recognising Clint as an American buyer with some track record. 'Six thousand, seven eight, ten, twelve, fifteen, twenty. At twenty thousand, twenty thousand, twenty thousand.' The auctioneer was going red in the face while he repeated the number like a broken record, as he looked directly at Bob Adam who was conferring with another man beside him. 'Is it, Bob? Another?' Bob Adam nodded. ''Twenty five thousand guineas.' He glanced around the whispering crowd before retuning his look to Clint Tomson who nodded his head again. 'Thirty thousand, thirty thousand,' repeated the auctioneer a grin on his face as the recognised the new breed record-price. He looked back to Bob Adam again, who this time shook his head. 'Thirty thousand it is then,' he squawked, just about to bang down his gavel. 'Is there anyone else,' Eddie made a show of having one last look around the crowd, ready to commit the sale, until he spotted someone waving a catalogue from the corner of his eye. The catalogue belonged to a Stetson hat which was on the head of a large man that he, and many others, recognised. Professionally, Eddie took a deep breath and started again. 'Thirty five.' Back to Tomson. 'Forty, forty five.' By now you could have heard a whisker of hay fall to the ground. 'Fifty, fifty five thousand, fifty five thousand.' Again he raised his gavel, before turning back to the man in the tweed suit. As one, the whole crowd held their breath and, for a second, so did the auctioneer, poised with hammer raised. Then came the final nod. 'Sixty thousand guineas!' Eddie looked back to Leachman who shook his head. 'Sixty thousand guineas, ladies and gentlemen, a new world record!' Clint mouthed something across the noisy sale ring and Eddie translated it. 'Goes to Black Watch Farms, New York!' The whole building erupted into a spontaneous round of applause.

Jack Dick, seated on a bench high up in the gallery, let out a smile, shaking Gar Douglas's hand next to him and shouting into his ear above the noise. 'I think we just hit the headlines!'

What he failed to add was that he had personally just

hit the jackpot as, by tomorrow, a percentage of this amount was just heading towards his own untraceable Swiss bank account, less the five hundred bucks he owed to Leachman!

Jack Dick left, shakes hands with Sir Torquil Munro. with Gar Douglas, Lady Munro and Clint Tomson behind

Lindertis Evulse 1963
World-record priced bull

# Newhouse, near Glamis Castle, Scotland - February 1963

'Gentlemen, welcome to our home, glad you could make it. Hope the weather wasn't too bad for you. That snow can be a bit tricky coming through the Drumochter pass.' Mrs Adam encouraged the two men inside out of the cold, both removing their hats and wiping their feet. 'I'll just fetch Bob, I think he is on the telephone.'

Jack surveyed the low ceilinged farmhouse kitchen, every wall adorned with photographs of Angus bulls and coloured rosettes. There were other animal pictures too, including Shorthorn cattle and a few different sheep. He closely inspected a picture of a Border Leicester ram, its ears nearly a foot long, with a note under it saying it had broken the breed record-price. It was evidence that here he was in the company of greatness, a man who was not only at the top of one breed, but one who could excel at breeding whatever livestock he touched. Jack considered the breed record price. This morning there would have been pictures on every newspaper in Britain of a bull that not only broke the record, but doubled it.

Gar Douglas was studying the pictures too, concentrating on the descriptions under the photographs, recognising bull names and men's faces. They had come here to buy some female Angus at Bob Adam's invitation and Gar was particularly excited by that. The day had already been spent touring another couple of cattle studs in the area and they had purchased a few cattle but he knew this was where the real gold was.

Bob appeared at the doorway. 'Jack, Gar, come on through by the fire.' The two men shook his hand. A crackling fire raged in the hearth of the living room driving out the colder air. In one corner a glass fronted cabinet filled half of a wall and was packed full of silver cups and salvers which reflected the orange glow of the fire whichever way you looked at it. Gar's eyes were drawn toward the impressive display but Jack was more interested in a large painting hung on the wall above the mantelpiece. Bob watched his eyes dwell on the print, an ancient picture of four cows with a castle in the background.

'I see you have an eye for fine art, Jack?'

'Indeed I do, Bob. Can you tell me about it?'

'The cattle are the original Ericas at Ballindalloch Castle, by David Steele, 1876.' Bob continued. 'Managed to buy it from J Earnest Kerr. You heard of him?'

Jack shook his head so Gar intervened, displaying his knowledge of the breed. 'Kerr of Harviestoun. Perhaps the greatest breeder this century. And Ballindalloch was the home of George MacPherson-Grant, one of the breed's founder-fathers. And your herd is built around the family of Erica cows, Mister Adam.'

Bob nodded his appreciation that at least one of these Americans had some knowledge of the origins of the Angus. 'Quite so, Gar, well done. Now gentlemen, down to business. A dram of whisky to warm you up?' He reached for a bottle of malt from the sideboard and three crystal glasses, pouring a two finger measure into each. 'And then let's go and look at some heifers.'

The snow was starting to fall again as the three men made their way across the yard to a white-washed stone-built cattle court. Steam rose from inside the building which was lit by a couple of dim light bulbs. Once through the door, Jack let Gar study the cattle while Bob engaged him in conversation. Adam was no fool, he knew that much, and he got the feeling that this man would try and play him like he played his own clients. It was a challenge he relished.

'These are all the females in here, some of the best breeding in Scotland. So, how many are you are looking for, Jack?' Bob rubbed his bare hands together, partly to keep the circulation going and partly in expectation of the good deal he was about to pull off.

'Bob.' Jack looked him in the eye, as his own eyes narrowed. 'I wanna buy the ones that are not for sale.' This made Bob splutter for a minute. 'No disrespect to Gar here,' he continued quietly, out of the other man's earshot, 'he might know his cattle, but I know people. So - what's that English expression? - let's not beat around the bush, Bob. You and I both know that you have another shed full of all your best stock around the corner some place.' Bob couldn't help but join in with that infectious smile, nodding his head in understanding that maybe he had underestimated his quarry.

Instead of denial Bob answered in an equally low voice. 'They'll be expensive!'

'Tell you what we do, Bob. Let Gar pick out ten of his favourites in this pen and you and me pick a couple of *your* favourites outta the other place. Then we will have a deal. We can spread the price across the lot. I get to keep the best ones for the Black Watch herd, and the others? Well, my investors will be more than happy to pay the full price for animals bred at Newhouse of Glamis, no matter how good they are. How's that sound?'

Again Bob nodded his head, slowly, and then suddenly clapped his hands. 'Come on Gentlemen. The night is closing in, and so is the weather. I have you a room booked in the hotel. These cattle will look much better in the daylight tomorrow.' With that he turned on his heels, heading back towards the house. A deal had been done.

An hour later the three men were huddled in the busy

bar of the Strathmore Arms, warmed by a roaring coal fire and the body heat of a dozen locals all engrossed in conversation, mainly about the day's shooting. Stags' heads with huge antlers spread out from the walls towards the yellowed ceiling.

They picked a table in the corner near the fire, as a couple of greenly-clad ruddy-faced men got up to leave, one acknowledging Bob with a single nod. For the next couple of hours Jack picked Bob's brains about breeding cattle and how he came to be so successful, over a few more malt whiskies. Bob told of how, as a young lad, he saved all his pocket money to pay for his first Angus cow and eventually got a chance to take a tenancy on Glamis estate, growing potatoes and selling them to the seed merchants down in England. Jack could relate to that story and mentioned how he paid his way through college by playing poker. The two men laughed at that. Large plates of steak and chips arrived, and went, as more whisky followed to wash it down. The conversation turned from cattle to sheep, and sheep to fine art as one by one the locals started to leave, most of them walking home as the snow built up outside. Gar had gone off to his room, bidding them goodnight and Jack was explaining that he was collecting British sporting paintings, mainly of horses, and was heading south the next day to an auction house near London hoping to pick up a couple. A thin young man stood on his own at the bar, nursing a near empty whisky glass, his red nose glowing, probably as a combination of spending too many days out in the cold coupled with too much drink. When it was his round, Bob signalled to the barman to put a drink in for Hamish and the young man turned around to think him. With a thin whiskery moustache and lank hair that covered his ears, Hamish spoke in an accent so broad that Jack was hardly able to interpret. Bob introduced them, explaining that Hamish was a local gamekeeper who occasionally did some work at his farm during the summer months. The family were from the hills around these parts and his father had worked as a shepherd for Brigadier Gordon on a neighbouring estate for all of his life, while his mother was the housekeeper there.

'I couldn't help over-hearing, Mister Bob, that this man was looking for some paintings of horses,' Hamish said, sheepishly. 'Only, when I was a boy, we used to play in the old barn at the back of the big hoos.' All locals referred to the Laird's main abode as the big house, generally an imposing stone-built castle with mice in the skirting boards and drafts from every window. 'I'm nae sure if it's still there, mind, but there used to be a big picture up in the attic there. It was of a man sitting on a horse and the horse had a short tail and spindly legs and I can remember thinking that he wannae win many races on legs like that!'

Jack's interest was sparked, so he asked, 'Was there a name on it?'

'Aye, I reckon there was, but it's been a while ago now.' The young man was thinking. 'Something to do with fish...? Haddock, maybe..'

Jack could barely contain his excitement as the whisky coursed through his veins. 'Herring, perhaps?'

'Aye, that'd be it, yes. Herring.'

Jack turned to Bob. 'How far is this place away?'

'Five, maybe six miles, why?'

Jack was already standing up to, leave. 'Come on Bob. Let's go and see it. No time to lose.'

Bob glanced firstly at the clock and then the snow outside, then down at the two full glasses of whisky still lined up on the table in front of him. 'At this hour?'

'No time like the present!' For a man who rarely drank, Jack had a surprisingly good hold of his whisky, as Bob, by far the larger man struggled to his feet and put a hand on the mantelpiece to steady himself. 'Can you drive,

Hamish?'

Within minutes, with Jack sitting in the centre seat, Bob on his left and Hamish behind the wheel, Bob's Land-rover pulled out of the car-park of the Strathmore arms, the time approaching midnight. It might have only been a five mile journey but, on a dark winter's night with falling snow, it took well over half an hour to reach the old castle as the wheels of the vehicle battled with the road and a few high hedges, the wipers struggling to keep the windscreen clear. Hamish had already telephoned the house from the payphone in the hotel, telling his mother that they were on their way, despite her protestation. A light was on as they pulled up the drive to the front door.

'I say,' said a booming voice through the snow, ' what the bloody hell is this all about? It's nearly midnight?'

Jack was out of the vehicle in no time, climbing out on Hamish's side rather than waking Bob who had fallen fast asleep on the way. He instructed the young man to leave the engine running and the heater on in the Land-rover. 'Don't want our man to freeze to death, now, do we?'

Bold as brass he walked up to the Brigadier who, he noticed to his discomfort was holding a shotgun under one arm. 'Jack Dick, New York,' he said holding out a hand to shake.

The older man looked down at his hand as though it was on fire. 'Dick, you say?'

'Yes, Sir. Come all the way from New York.'

'Well, you had better come in, dear boy.' The Brigadier was dressed in heavy tweed trousers and a cloak across his shoulders, all that was missing from the attire was a deer-stalker hat, and Jack suspected he usually wore one in daylight hours. He lowered his gun and shook Jack's hand. 'Any relation to the Dick's from Stirling?'

Jack assumed the role of Scottish ancestry. 'My father's

uncle,' he lied, admiring the size of the great hallway. Within minutes, the two of them were sitting in heavy leather chairs by a rekindled fire that the housekeeper had just lit, its crackles echoing around the draughty old room as shadows danced on the walls like ghouls at a barn dance. A layer of snow was spreading itself along the old stone floor, driving under the door as if trying to reach the fire itself.

'Something about a painting, was it?' The Brigadier accepted a tumbler of whisky that the housekeeper offered him, even though he had not asked her to. Jack took one as well. The old man's voice was aristocratic English, with just hint of Scottish twang. 'Got a few of the bloody things around the place. My grand-father used to collect them. Not really my thing. More of a shooting and fishing man, myself.' He studied the American looking around the walls. 'Do you fish, Dick?'

Jack turned back to the conversation. 'Marlin,' he said.

'Good god, man. That's not fishing, being strapped into a boat on the sea!' Jack thought the old man was going to explode. 'Can't beat a quiet day on the Tay with a few flies. Salmon, boy! That's what it's about. Got to pitch your wits against the blighters.'

'About the painting, Sir. Young Hamish said you had one in the attic in the barn,' said the American, considering that pitching his wits against this old buffoon would be a doddle compared to some of the deals he had done.

'Ah yes, there is one up there. Never liked it much.'

'Can I see it?'

Then old man drew in a long wheezy breath. 'Can't it wait until tomorrow?'

'Sorry, Sir. Have to be on a plane first thing in the morning.'

'Oh, alright. Hamish will show you the way.'

Minutes later, Jack was following Hamish up a half

rotten ladder in the barn, a dim flashlight in his hand. By the time he reached the old attic, Hamish has was already unwrapping the painting, and dusting it off. Jack shone his torch towards it, illuminating a large canvas in a wooden frame depicting a tall dark horse standing on green grass against a greying sky. 'Amato, you beauty,' he said quietly to himself.

'Is it the sort of thing you are looking for, Sir?' Hamish asked, his breath coming out in clouds in the cold night air.

Inside, Jack's heart was pounding as he coolly said, 'Well, it's not very valuable, but bring it down anyway.' He didn't need to study it any further, as he went to head back down the ladder. 'And be careful with it!'

Back in the main house, the old man was snoring by the fire when Jack coughed to announce his arrival.

'What?' Brigadier Gordon opened his eye. 'Well Dick? Is it of any interest?' The old man stood unsteadily to his feet.

Jack repeated what he said to Hamish. 'And not in very good condition either. But I'll take it off your hands, if you like?'

The ex-army man pulled himself up to his full height and Jack was quite surprised how tall he was. 'Is it worth two hundred pounds...?' The old man tailed off, watching Jack's eyes.

Too many games of poker had taught Jack not to show emotion when doing a deal. 'I guess it is, maybe.' He smiled.

Thunder appeared from nowhere in Gordon's eyes and his voice boomed it out. 'Well, if you say it's worth two hundred, and you have driven here in the middle of the night from New bloody York.' He stopped for breath. 'Then it must be worth at least a thousand!'

Thirty minutes later, Jack unwrapped the painting once more, this time in the comfort of his own hotel room, not believing his luck that he had not only just secured a John Herring painting, but his finest work: 'Amato, Royal Derby winner, 1838'. And for a fraction of its value!

## New York Supreme Court - April 1963

At nearly 60 years old, Louis J Lefkowitz had been around the block a few times. Born to a Jewish father and mother, he had grown up during the depression in Manhattan and believed he had seen it all. Elected to the New York state assembly in 1928, he had become Attorney General in 1957 after his predecessor, Jacob Javits, had been elected to the US Senate. With still yet higher aspirations, he had stood for Mayor of New York in 1961 but had been narrowly defeated. Some say this left him a bitter man.

It had been back in 1960 that Lefkowitz had first had reason to prosecute Jack Dick, when the Securities Commission brought the man's dealings to his attention. At the time he had been using money from a joint venture with a few traders to buy a steel company for $1.5m. With little cash to invest himself, Jack had put up the shares that he owned in the company as collateral for the deal. When the deal fell apart because the financial company which he had been hiding behind went out of business, nearly all 30 of Jack's partners in the deal had sued him and the attorney general was forced to review the case. It hadn't taken long to establish that Dick had made false guarantees to his investors and the resulting prosecution had barred him from trading securities in New York.

Their next encounter had been a year later when it was uncovered that Jack had been using a false name, that of his friend John Moritz, to buy 300,000 dollars worth of stocks because he knew the brokerage firms would never sell to him directly. Despite his protestations that he had Moritz's permission, this time it resulted in the Federal

Court banning him from any further violations of antifraud regulations.

'Mister Dick, we meet again!' Lefkowitz glowered down at Jack, his glasses on the end of his nose as the man's receding hairline reflected the spot lights on his forehead. Dick remained silent.

Over the course of the next five minutes, the AG read out his case, stating that Jack had been attempting to raise securities in New York for his latest sordid little scheme and this in itself was a violation of the injunction against him. This was countered by Jack's lawyer stating that the company of Black Watch was not in Dick's own name but that of his wife's brother, Richard Terker, also a New York attorney. On hearing this Lefkowitz raised his eyebrows and moved on to the next issue.

Black Watch Farms had been attempting to defraud public investors with its published financial statements claiming false evidence of their assets. In short it had omitted to disclose that the company was encumbered by mortgages and that it owed $250,000 on its herds. Furthermore, there was also no mention that of the 1 million dollar capital paid into the scheme so far, Black Watch had siphoned off $177,000 in commissions and expenses.

After a lengthy discussion from both sides, Lefkowitz slapped an injunction on the company to withdraw its falsified circular information, as well as imposing a 15,000 dollar fine. In his closing statement, he proffered the words, 'I will be watching you closely, Mister Dick!'

Unshaken, Jack left the building via the back entrance, not wanting to face a few of the local press who had taken an interest in the case.

## New York International Airport - May 1963

'One at a time, please. One at a time.' Jack straightened his tie and blinked in the spotlights, looking out over the sea of news reporters and smiling to the cameras. 'The plane will be arriving any minute, so I can't give you much time.' This was of course a lie, Jack had all the time in the world to feed the National Press and the whole thing had been very professionally stage managed by Stan Irwin, using the same promotion company that worked with TV's Johnny Carson. 'Yes, Sir. You.' He pointed.

'Mister Dick? Claude Sitton, New York Times. Can you explain why this bull was so expensive?'

'Expense is all relative, Mister Sitton. You say he was expensive, I say 176,000 dollars is a fair price. If you want the best, you gotta outbid the rest.'

'Are you saying he is the best bull in the world?' Sitton continued.

'Hell, yes.' Jack smiled and moved on to another reporter, as a snigger of laughs echoed around the small room. 'Lindertis Evulse. Make sure you get the spelling correct.'

A young fresh-faced man in a sheepskin coat with greasy hair called out, 'Mister Dick? Who will the bull belong to?'

'Black Watch Farms, Wappingers Falls, New York. We are a cattle farming enterprise backed by a number of investors, who are looking for a return on their dollar. When we put this bull to 'service' over the very best of our cows, my investors will reap the profit several times over.'

Another man called out. 'Can you tell me who your

investors are, Sir?'

Jack was ready for this one. 'Just ordinary people, like you and me, Son. Trying to make their dollar go further in this shrinking society.'

The man backed up his question. 'Would it be right to say your scheme can help people avoid paying tax?

'Have you seen the tax rate out there? Man, it's like the tale of Robin Hood - except the government is taking from the rich and giving to the, er, government!' Jack brought on another laugh from the crowd. '91% tax, that means you only get to keep nine cents in the dollar.'

The reporter was continuing, saying that was only if you earned over $200,000 per year but Jack had moved on to another question.

'Legal? Of course it's legal,' he smiled. 'Do I look like the sort of guy who would be doing something illegal?' With that the rumble of an airplane shook the building and Jack grinned. 'Gotta go, Gentlemen. Looks like the cargo has landed.' Slipping out through the back door, Jack was met by Irwin. 'Everything set?' he asked.

The man nodded. 'All in place, Jack.'

Jack watched the cargo plane taxi up the runway toward the big hanger, BOAC displayed on its side in huge lettering. 50 yards away, the hungry press were penned back behind barriers, all itching to get a look at the animal. Since they had purchased him the bull had been shipped to Ireland and held in quarantine for three months, which was to do with new regulations around a British outbreak of foot and mouth disease. Jack had made sure it had been well looked after during that time, paying for a young man to travel with the bull as its personal keeper. He made his way over to the hanger, covering his ears as the giant plane's jet engines whirred at 10,000 rpm. By the time he got there, the noise had died down a little and he caught up with Gar Douglas who was filling in some paperwork.

'All in order, Gar?' he shouted, looking over his shoulder. Gar nodded. Already the rear ramp of the Boeing 707 was being lowered. First down the ramp was a young man he recognised, the one who had been appointed to travel with the bull. Jack approached him. 'Welcome to America, Son. How is Evulse?'

'He's looking fine, Mister Dick. He did catch a bit of a chill a few weeks back, but he's fine now.' He accepted the baseball cap that Jack was proffering to him, embroidered with Black Watch Farms across the front.

'Well, you stay with him. Mr Irwin there will explain what to do.'

With that, Jack stood back and watched the show. One of Irwin's staff was allowing the press photographers nearer to the building, cordoning them off from the plane and the runway with a length of white tape. As one the throng surged forward, snapping away at a large crate which was being slowly wheeled off the back of the aircraft. The grey box sat on the tarmac for a good five minutes, building up the intensity of the situation, while clips were undone and clipboards were completed. On his cue, Jack walked across to the reporters, calling out above their chattering noise.

'Gentlemen. I give you Lindertis Evulse, the world's most expensive bull!' Jack waved his arm towards the plane as though introducing Johnny Carson himself. With that he moved back, as two men rolled out a red carpet, starting near the plane and ending somewhere towards the reporters. Again, on cue, a security wagon revved its engine, tearing around the corner of the building, its blue lights flashing on top. The worlds Brinks Mat were written on the side, possibly America's most high profile secure cash and bullion delivery service. Once positioned near the carpet, a signal was sent and the door to the box opened, as Kevin tugged on a white rope halter. As the first glimpse of the bull immerged, dozens of flashbulbs popped, lighting up the whole area. Slightly reluctant at first, Evulse was led up the middle of the red carpet as though arriving at an Oscar award ceremony, his back coat glistening with sweat as the flashing lights illuminated him. With a little more persuasion, he was shoehorned into the back of the waiting truck. Once the door was closed, again on cue, four Harley-Davidson motor bikes arrived around the corner, flanking the vehicle on all sides. As one the whole cavalcade set off, arcing around the tarmac towards the exit, lights flashing and sirens wailing.

Watching it disappear, at least a dozen reporters ran across to Jack, throwing up more questions which he handled with capable ease.

## Wappingers Falls Ranch - July 1963

'What's up, Gar?' Jack glanced up from his desk and could immediately see that his main cattleman was the bearer of bad news. Gar handed him a sheet of paper and Jack studied it.

Eventually he stood up and said, 'Are you sure? I don't understand. He was good when we bought him. What went wrong?'

'Had two independent tests, both came back the same. The bull's not working, Jack.' Gar was pacing the office. 'Something must have happened when he was in Ireland.'

Jack checked the test results on the sheet of paper again, shaking his head. 'This is going to make us look very foolish, Gar.'

'You think I don't know that. World's most expensive bull, shooting blanks!'

'Have you spoken to the breeder?'

'Sure, I phoned him last night. John Rugg says that the bull was tested by vets in Edinburgh, and his semen was said to be OK.' Gar took off his hat and sat down. 'So I spoke to the veterinary surgery. They say that when Evulse went to Perth sale they tried to take semen from him to test but the bull was too young, not mature enough to get a sample. After we bought him and Rugg took the bull home, one of the vets visited the farm and took another sample and that was the one that tested good.'

Jack considered this. 'What are you saying Gar. That the sample they tested was not from our bull. A case of mistaken identity?' Jack slammed his fist down on the desk and shouted. 'That they fucked us over?' Jack was reaching for the telephone.

'Hang on there, Jack. I'm not saying anything. Maybe it was, maybe it wasn't. Young Kevin said the bull caught a chill when he was in Ireland. Maybe it was that. Maybe it was the drugs they gave him. Who knows?' Gar's voice calmed down. 'There ain't no proof, Jack.'

Dick sat back down in his seat, looking up to the ceiling, thinking. To most men, this would have proved a complete disaster, something that would take a long time to recover from. But not Jack R Dick.

After a few seconds a smile came to his face and he stood up again, searching in a filing cabinet. He pulled out a box file and sat down again, sorting through some of the papers until he found what he was looking for. Gar looked at the paper upside down, making out the heading, LLOYDS OF LONDON, while Jack checked it through, nodding his head. The smile broadened and Gar grinned too.

'He's insured against infertility, isn't he, Jack?' It was a statement rather than a question.

Two or three phone calls later, Jack had the situation back under control. The insurance company Lloyds, had agreed to refund the entire purchase price of 174,000 dollars assuming they could appoint their own vets to make the test. The more Jack considered this, the more he realised he had once again been dealt an exceptionally good hand. By buying a bull in Scotland for a record price, he had secured the attention of the world's press, which in turn had brought in loads of enquiries and certainly added some confidence to his existing clients. Now he could reclaim the entire price and spend it again. It wasn't as though the stud was short of stock bulls. As well as buying Lindertis Evulse at the Perth sale, Jack had also invested in the day's supreme champion, Escort of Manorhill. The bull had arrived a few weeks earlier and was now settled in his own surroundings at the ranch. Escort was the second

Perth Grand Champion at Black Watch as they already had Elavate of Eastfield, previous record price holder. Some of his calves were looking promising, even he could see that, and Gar was more than pleased with them.

When Gar had left the office, Jack picked up the phone again, this time to his buddy and advisor, Lester Leachman. He explained the situation to him and then asked a simple question, the real reason he had called. 'You know most of the veterinaries in this area, you think any of them might be able to get the bull firing again?' Jack listened and then waited a while, as the line went quiet and eventually he picked up a pen, scribbling down a name. 'Thanks, Les. Speak later.'

Next morning, a man in a suit arrived from Lloyds of London's New York office, accompanied by a vet and his assistant. Over the next hour they managed to coax a vial of semen from Lindertis Evulse. Black Watch had recently set up its own laboratory in a new built barn at the far end of the stud. Using their facilities, the vet put the sample under a microscope and confirmed what they already knew. Back in his office, the representative went through the paperwork with Jack and one of the office girls, completing a long form which they both signed at the bottom and then being informed that the money would be back in Black Watch bank account within five days. 'Nice doing business with you, Mister.' As the man was about to leave, Jack gave him a smile. 'Say, now you own my bull, what do you intend to do with him?' he asked. The man looked blank for a while and then revealed that the usual practice was to get the vet to shoot him, here and now, and then dispose of the carcass. Jack feigned just enough sympathy to sound convincing. 'Aw, such a shame. It's not the bull's fault his nuts don't work. And he travelled half across the world. What say you leave him here as a showpiece?'

The man was protesting that the animal was now

property of Lloyds of London and that wouldn't be possible. Eventually, after some persuasion, he gave Jack the phone number of one of the insurance underwriters in London. As they couldn't be reached at this time of day in England, Jack requested that the veterinary surgeon leave the bull for now and, if he could not strike a deal, the man could come back tomorrow with his gun.

By 3pm, and a number of phone calls put on hold, Jack eventually got a call through to the man he needed to speak to. A two minute conversation, with Jack doing most of the talking, and a deal had been struck and he managed to buy the bull back off the company. For one dollar!

## Williamsburg, Brooklyn - Fall 1963

Jack pressed the doorbell, looking around at the neighbourhood he knew as a kid. It had surprised him how things had changed in what seemed like a short time, where some of the old boarded-up brick terraced properties were now turned into swanky houses as the whole area had been developed. 'Maybe I should have gone into real-estate,' he thought to himself, nodding to a good looking young couple exiting the house next door.

'Jack, great to see you.' Steve Lawrence swung the door wide, stepping out to give Jack a big hug. 'You haven't changed a bit. Come in.'

Jack eyed his old school pal. They hadn't been close as kids but had played football together at Jefferson High. Back then he had known him as Sidney Liebowitz, a Jewish kid from a Jewish community, although the boy had always mixed in with the rest, and was a hit with the girls. After school they lost contact, when Sidney was drafted into the army. Since then, when he came back to NYC he had changed his name to Steve Lawrence and had somehow gotten in to the music business. After that he spent a lot of time out of town. Jack caught a glimpse of him on TV from time, usually dressed in a trademark white suit, crooning his hit songs on some show or other. Today he was just wearing brown pants and a woollen jumper and Jack thought he looked just like another regular guy. Shorter than he remembered, too.

'Drink?' Lawrence turned to him from a walnut veneered cocktail cabinet, laden with crystal decanters. He wondered if, once fame had gone to his head, Steve was taking a little too much out of the bottle for himself.

'Scotch, thanks.' Jack took a seat on the sofa, its buttoned leather smelled brand new and reminded him of his days in the furniture business, selling people three piece suites wrapped up as dreams. On the wall a few works of art, mainly modern stuff, briefly caught his attention, although it wasn't Jack's style. 'Doing well for yourself, these days, Steve?' He accepted the glass, still finding it hard to call the man by his made-up name, as he sat down beside him.

'Ah well, you know. Had a few hits, gotten on TV, I suppose some would say it's not a bad life but..' he sipped at his drink. 'We're out on the road too much these days. Town after town, hotel after hotel. It's not all it's cracked up to be. Did I tell you I got married?'

'Yeah, last time I bumped into you at the 21 club. Wife's a singer too huh?'

'She ain't just a singer, Jack, she is a great singer. We are doing some stuff together.' He glanced up at a picture of them both over the fireplace, a microphone each, facing each other. 'Best thing that ever happened to me.' A smile came to his lips, raising his cheek bones.

Jack could see why he was a star, with those good looks. And her too! Eydie Gorme had been a sensation before the two had met and a heartthrob of most American men. The newspapers had called them the perfect couple, as their wedding picture made the headlines a few years back. A lesser man would have been jealous.

'So what about you, Jack? You never said what you came to see me about?' Steve turned to face him. 'If you're here to sell me some furniture, I already got some new stuff a few weeks back.'

Jack let out a chuckle. 'Nah, that game was never really for me.' He reached for his briefcase. 'These days I am in the farming business!'

It was Steve's chance to let out a laugh, as he nearly

choked on his drink. 'You, a farmer!' he spluttered. 'Aw come on, Jack, now I heard it all. You are a city boy, through and through.'

'It's true, Steve. Got me a place out in the sticks these days. Big old farmhouse, rolling fields full of cows. All the fresh air you can eat.'

Steve looked at him again, expecting a punch line, which didn't come, so he completed one himself. 'Well, you can take the man out of New York, but you can't take New York out the man.' Steve accepted a brochure that Jack was proffering to him. 'What's this?'

'Steve, I figured you must be making a lotta money these days?' Jack put on a concerned face, 'and then give a whole heap of it back to the Government.' Steve's eyes confirmed the latter so he continued. 'What if I told I had a way you could save all that tax, and then get to spend it on your family?'

'I'd say it was probably illegal!' Steve broke a smile. 'Only kidding, Jack. Come on, you and I go way back. How does this go? I give you money and you bury it in the ground? Or put it on a horse?'

Jack kept his charm offensive. 'No, Steve. Not on a horse. On a cow!' Then came the winning smile. 'You and Eydie get to buy your own herd of cows, and I look after them for you. You can visit them whenever you want. We're only an hour away from here.'

'Are you aware how nuts that just sounded?' Steve grinned as Jack nodded. 'You're serious, right? I get to be a farmer too, just like you?' He glanced at Jack's attire, in his dark suit, tie, shiny shoes and briefcase. Then he stopped and went silent for a while. This was the part that Jack liked the best. Feed them a line and then let it sink in. Never break that moment. Eventually, the question came. The one he could answer in short, to close the deal. 'And what's in it for me, Jack?'

## Governor's Office, Birmingham, Alabama, June 1963

George Wallace sat at his desk, looking down at the latest newspaper headlines. Unrest in the state was reaching fever pitch as the problems with racial uprising escalated. For every rally that gathered in public and then got broken up by the police, more photos of bloodshed and state brutality hit the front pages.

In his earlier years as a county court judge, he had taken a liberal stance against the black community, making informed decisions based on fairness, despite colour or creed. However, when it came to running for governor, this cut no ice with the white voters and he had failed to secure the seat in 1958. It wasn't until he had stood up against Martin Luther King, almost making a political u-turn, and started quoting how segregation of blacks and whites was the only way forward that, in November 1962, he had managed to win the nomination and then secure a crushing victory. Since then, Governor Wallace had stood up to President Kennedy who was making a stand towards integrating blacks and whites, particularly in educational establishments such as the University of Alabama.

'Yes, Mary,' he agitatedly snapped down the phone. 'Who? Jack R Dick, New York. The hell he want?' He was about to decline the call when curiosity got the better of him. 'OK, put him through.'

'Congratulations on your appointment as Governor, George. You are doing a fine job down there in the south.' Wallace listened as Jack proffered his smooth talking. 'Hope you don't mind me calling but a mutual associate of ours suggested I get in touch. I have a rare opportunity for you to do something for the black's, Sir!

'That's kinda doubtful, but I'm listening,' sniffed the Governor.

'Sir, this one will probably hit the National papers tomorrow. This black we have in mind is in need of some treatment, and the only place it can happen is in Alabama!' Jack paused for effect, to let the man take in the information.

'Well, who is this son of a bitch?'

'Actually, Sir. It is not a who, but a what. I am talking about an Aberdeen Angus!'

George Wallace's face turned a bright shade of red. 'Why you bastard! How dare you phone me with a load of bull!'

## Auburn University Veterinary School, Alabama - October 1963

Jack smiled to himself as they drove through the University campus. Only months earlier, Tuscaloosa University had been splashed all over the news, with JFK himself paying a visit trying to diffuse controversy over allowing two black students to enroll. The Governor was on the wrong end of that one but, after a second phone call, and then some follow-up from a few news hounds, George Wallace saw the opportunity to try and make a few amends this time around.

Auburn had gained reputation as one of the outstanding veterinary schools in the whole south, overseen by Professor Donald Walker, a top surgeon of Scottish descent. Under Jack's request, endorsed by Governor Wallace, Walker had assembled a group of 17 surgeons, doctors, medical students, including one black one, who had been briefed on the task that they had to perform. 'It was a long shot,' weren't odds that Jack Dick was afraid of. Much of his business life he had taken a punt on long shots.

As they neared the university hospital, Jack riding passenger in a large semi truck, he spotted a number of TV News vans lined up on the road outside, again being organised by the ever inventive Stan Irwin. What he was a little more surprised to see were a couple of female students holding up a large banner saying 'Good luck Lindy!' In fact, hundreds of students had assembled a welcoming committee for him. The name Lindy had been invented by a member of the press, possibly because the spelling of Lindertis Evulse varied with every publication.

And, since his arrival in New York some months back, Lindy had certainly pulled in a lot of column inches.

Using his ever growing slick publicity machine, Jack had drip fed stories of Lindy's progress to the press, stating that he had been put on a strict diet to shed 300 pounds from his now 1800 pound frame in a hope it would increase his sexual performance. This had partly been true, on the advice of Professor Walker who had taken a personal interest in the animal, after a couple of other establishments had failed in their attempts to rectify his issue. Walker had performed such an operation 6 times on other animals in the last couple of years, with two being successful.

Headlines such as 'THE DUD STUD' and 'THE LACKLUSTRE LOTHARIO' had almost immortalised the bull and his plight. Since the first announcement of his virility problem, Evulse had received letters of encouragement and even fan mail. To appease the ever hungry press, Jack had produced pictures of the bull in his own comfortable surroundings at Black Watch, complete with overhead fans to keep him cool. Suggestions that they had tried all sorts of medicines and potions to help him out with his sexual prowess had enhanced his profile yet further. Esquire Magazine had even put his picture on their front cover, a place usually reserved for the rich and famous. Although most of the stories included the words 'laughing stock,' Jack saw it as anything but. If they could do a successful operation, he would now have a world record and world famous bull at stud which cost him just one dollar! Admittedly he would have to pay for the operation, which didn't come cheap, but the publicity he was gaining was worth 100 times that. In fact, Jack had already done a deal on payment with the head of the University, Dr Hicks, persuading him that if Evulse did get to produce valuable semen, Hicks would get a third share of the sale rights, although he failed to mention in the small-print he had added to the contract that only included sales in Alabama state!

Local police cleared their path as the large semi-trailer swung around in front of the main doors to the hospital, where a ramp had been built. Amid a barrage of flashbulbs, Evulse emerged down the ramp of the lorry, led by Jack himself. The wooden ramp creaked quite unsteadily under the bull's weight although this couldn't be heard amongst the spontaneous round of applause that had erupted from the crowd on their first sighting of the famed animal. Carpets had been especially laid along the route through a long corridor on what would have been an otherwise slippery tiled floor.

Once inside, a selected number of journalists were also allowed into the operating room, each one kitted out with hygiene robes and masks. A giant metal frame was in the centre of the room and Evulse, now quite used to being centre of public attention, was persuaded to step inside. From then on, the room was ushered to silence as the anaesthetist administered a large dose of anaesthetic and the crowd waited. Leather straps were fastened under the animal's belly which strained under his weight once the beast's legs started to buckle. Professor Walker, like something from an alien B-movie, pulled a handle and the whole crate turned toward the horizontal with a slow whirring noise. Once the crate was on its side, the outer bars were removed so that it was just one large operating table. A couple of surgeons started working with hair clippers around the great bull's testicles, while a few cameras snapped away.

Jack left the room at this point, catching a cup of coffee in the canteen before heading outside to brief the press on the latest progress. While he had been inside, under his instruction a couple of workers had erected four makeshift pens out of steel gates which they had brought with them on the lorry. They were also told not to speak to anyone about what they were doing. Jack would have plenty of time, with the operation scheduled to take up to three hours, so he took the opportunity to make a couple of phone calls from Professor Walker's office.

Like any other major hospital the veterinary school was kitted out with some of the most modern equipment available. Air conditioning cooled the inside air and an overhead fan swirled the smell of disinfectant around the room. Tiles on the floor looked like they were scrubbed three times a day, they were so slick. A row of chairs at one side of the room were positioned behind a plate glass window, giving the reporters a perfect view of the room, as they eagerly watched the surgeons at work.

At least half a dozen reporters he recognised were waiting outside, smoking cigarettes and chatting to each other.

'Mister Dick, any news yet?'

Jack considered that the anticipation was like waiting for a baby to be born, except with a dozen expectant fathers. 'They are making good progress, and the patient is currently asleep,' he proffered. Looking around he spotted one of the young cattlemen who had travelled down in the lorry with the animals, Jack having opted to fly and be collected at Birmingham airport. He gave the young man a nod, who then went up into the back of the lorry.

'However,' Jack continued, 'when he wakes up, he may be looking for his first conquest.' With that, four young black heifers were driven down the ramp and positioned, one each, in the four pens that had been erected. 'These animals are four of Black Watch Farms most prized females. When Lindy comes out, he will have the opportunity to take his pick!' All the reporters were frantically writing while a couple of eager ones took photographs. 'As soon as we hear that the operation has been successful, you folks will be the first to know and have the chance to report it to the nation,' Jack continued.

Another hour passed before Jack appeared again, this

time not with quite the grin that he had been wearing earlier. Some of the reporters that had been inside the hospital followed him to the steps as he held out a sheet of paper and read from it.

'Lindertis Evulse, the world's most expensive and, dare I say, famous bull has undergone an operation today, under the supervision of Professor Donald Walker. The surgery conducted was to remove a blockage in his tubes, thought be the cause of his fertility problems. Professor Walker intimates that the two hour ordeal has been a success as far as he can estimate. Only time will tell if this is the case.' Behind him, the large black frame of the bull himself lumbered into view, as more flashbulbs popped in front of him. 'Gentlemen, please do not frighten the animal, he has just been through a rather uncomfortable procedure. '

Led by one of the veterinary students wearing a white smock, Evulse descended the wooded ramp, stopping to sniff at one of the heifers tied up next to a railing. Still looking rather groggy around the eyes, he then pulled his head back and raised his top lip, making the brass ring in his nose stand vertically. More photos were taken as he took a look at the other animals, then lay down and went to sleep!

## Wappingers Falls - January 1964

'Another farm, Jack. That's three we have now.' Gar Douglas, a moderate and quiet man, wasn't in the best of moods after Jack's announcement of the expansion to the Black Watch operation.

'Victims of our own success, Gar.' He smiled at his right hand man. 'Looks like everyone wants to play ball!'

'I'm just not sure I can run the numbers of cattle you are talking about. We have over 500 cows now, and an army of men. The new artificial insemination facility is going well at Fishkill, and that young English kid you took on seems to know what he is doing.' Gar stopped to consider his words, raising his eyebrows, and then calming down a little. 'We are starting to struggle to keep up the paperwork, Jack. Every cow is recorded in a ledger, and each calf has its own record, but that all takes staff time. My wife Patti has been doing most of the records, but if you take on another farm, and another 200 head like you are planning to, we are going to need at least two folk full time keeping records.'

Jack said. 'Once we get the lease to this Roosevelt farm, I want you to personally oversee it for 6 months until it is up and running. Then we will put a manager in there, and possibly here. And you get a raise and promoted to...' Jack looked to the ceiling for inspiration, 'how about vice President of Cattle Development?' He stopped to let the information set it before continuing. 'And I have been thinking about the paperwork side of it too. So that's why I got us a computer...!'

Having taken in his new title, Gar's mouth dropped open a second time. 'A computer. Jeez, Jack. We are farmers, not scientists!' he paced the room. 'How we going to learn all about that stuff.'

'All taken care of. The machine will sit in facility in NYC and we have two guys working the pedals. It has a brain the size of three whole rooms, and can remember millions of details, all at once. All you have to do is fill in the information in the right place and they will feed it in. Think about it, Gar. These things can do the work of 20 clerks.'

Gar was thinking about it. It would be like those science fiction films they made in Hollywood, with men in white coats pressing buttons and making pinging noises. Oh well, as long as he didn't have to use the thing himself. 'So we give them the records, and they fire us what in return?'

'Whatever you want, Gar. Stock lists, calving records, weight sheets. Hell, Gar, you just ask for it, and they will send it right across.' Jack stood to his feet, patting his man on the back. 'Welcome to the twenty first century, Gar!'

## Perth auction mart, Scotland - February 1964

'And you're sure this test is right,' Gar Douglas was asking. 'Only we had a few problems…'

Vic Findlay nodded that he was more than sure. 'We tried him out on a couple of cows, few months back, and he got them in calf.'

Gar looked the bull over once again. 'Damn fine animal,' he said quietly to himself. 'Boss says I gotta buy the grand champion, whatever it takes. Got two in the stable already, but he wants a third one.'

Vic tried not to look too pleased with this snippet of information. Essedium of Douneside certainly was one of the best bulls in the mart. The judge had awarded him champion and commented that he was the best bull the man had ever seen. Only once before had Essedium been exhibited in the public eye, at a small show near his home in Aberdeenshire. The bull had been beaten that day by a young rival but, cometh the hour - cometh the beast, Essedium had reversed the tables on that one now, pushing him into second place. Now here he was, potentially securing his passage to USA.

Douneside Estate in Tarland, Aberdeenshire belonged to the McRobert family. Or at least it used to. Lady MacRobert, herself an American, had married into the family, only to lose her husband shortly afterwards. The 12,000 acre estate was to be farmed by her three sons but, unfortunately, World War II broke out and all three went off to fly planes for the British Air Force. Sadly, none of them returned, leaving her ladyship not only widowed but without an heir. The sadness of the affair broke her heart and the whole farm was put into a trust to be run by some learned managers. However, the Aberdeen Angus herd had been continued, more recently with Vic in charge, and as a lover of animals, Lady MacRobert took a personal interest in the cattle. Over the next decade or so, some clever and expensive bull purchases had propelled the herd to one of the best in Scotland, with their genetics being in demand. Indeed it had been a cow from the Douneside herd that had been grandmother to Lindertis Evulse.

Essedium was much admired by many and it was fairly obvious that he was going to make a good price. However, not even in Vic's wildest dreams had he believed that his bull would chalk up the second top price in history as once again Clint Tomson did the bidding on behalf of Black Watch Farms, this time closing the deal at 54,000 guineas.

As the well-known auctioneer knocked his hammer down for the final time he remarked 'you are making a habit of this, Mister Dick!' What the watching crowd had failed to notice was that, once the bidding went above 25,000, the auctioneer had possibly been taking every other bid from a small dog seated in the third row, until an agreed price of 54,000 was reached!

Once again the top priced animal headed to New York, although this time the press were getting a little tired of being played like a fiddle by Jack and his PR people.

## The State office, South Carolina - February 1964

'Good to hear from you, Jack.' The well-known Senator glanced up at his PA sitting across the desk, indicating for her to leave him in peace with this phone call. 'How's the cattle business?' he continued. 'Or more to the point, how is my investment?' The Senator listened for a few minutes as Jack brought him up to speed. 'Well, Dwight seems kinda interested in the deal too, although we might want to keep that quiet just now?'

Jack was assuring absolute confidentiality, as with all his clients, but he was still a bit sceptical. 'OK, Jack. I hear ya. But, same as me, if Eisenhower puts some dollars in, you don't get to use his name anywhere, that understood?' The senior Senator listened some more. 'A favour. Really, Jack, you want ME to do you a favour?'

Patiently he listened as Jack made a case. 'Last year, when we bought those bulls in Scotland, we got a guy to ride with them to Ireland and he did a great job looking after them. Well. When the plane picked them up, he ended coming the whole way to New York.' Jack let the information sink in. 'The kid has worked cattle in Scotland and knows a helluva lot about the breed. Now my main cattleman has taken a shine to him and the boy has been staying over at his place.'

'You're gonna tell me this kid has no passport, right?' Gore raised his eyes. 'Goddammit, Jack. Why the hell do you get yourself on the wrong side of the law so much?'

'He just needs a work permit, my friend?'

'You know how hard those things are to get these days?' The Senator was shouting down the phone. 'Especially for Limeys. Gotta do interviews, run it by the state department. All sorts of rules out there now.'

'Not if you're the Senator..' Jack knew this was stepping over the mark, but the young lad had proven a good asset and the other hands were learning from him every day. 'I am sure your cows could have a few extra calves next year.'

At last the Senator let out a big sigh. 'Send me the details, I'll see what I can do. You're not gonna tell me has a criminal record too, are ya!'

# Black Watch Arabian Horse stud - September 1964

For all he rarely rode a horse, Jack had a passion for the creatures nearly as much as did about art. The first Arabian horses arrived at Wappingers Falls in 1964, three mares, one with a foal at foot. Every morning Jack would visit the horse paddock, admiring the slender animals with their athletic frames and high spirits. Before long, seeing the animals himself was no longer enough and his quest for breeding champions and top prices became as much an obsession as the cattle had done a few years earlier. What he needed was an expert.

Hailing from Cincinnati, Ohio, Bill Bohl had worked for renowned Arabian horse breeder, Bob Hart, before he took the job as trainer at Black Watch Arabian Stud, in 1965. Aged just 18, Bill already had a near encyclopaedic knowledge of the breed and a great eye for the beasts themselves. An energetic and eager young man, Jack believed this boy had what it would take to get Black Watch on the Arabian horse map.

As with everything else Jack touched, what started out as a hobby developed very quickly through a passing interest to an out-and-out business in its own right. To him, like all his other enterprises, his horses were a way of making money. It just so happened that Arab horses were coming into fashion around that time in the US and, along with Bohl, Black Watch sought out some of the best breeding stock he could find. If they were going play this game, they had to use the highest stakes.

Again, for Jack it wasn't about the horses; he was in the people business. He had read about breeder Bill

Munson, who was probably the top man in the US when it came to Arab and Quarter horses, and had put through a phone call. Not only a superb breeder, Munson was also a practising veterinarian, show judge, importer, rancher, pubic speaker and all round good guy with the gift of the gab. In Bill, Jack saw himself.

'Howdy, Bill, how was the ride?' Jack greeted Munson with a smile as he stepped down from the twin-engine aircraft with the letters BW on the door.

'As far as flying crates go, she was fairly steady.' The man smoothed down his hair and pulled his hat back on. 'But I'd rather ride in a saddle any day!'

Soon the pair were riding up front of the Chevy pick-up, heading from the makeshift runway towards the farm. As they drew near a couple of young horses were being schooled, trotting round and round the paddock on the end of long reigns.

'I don't know how you guys stay on those things,' Jack said, laughing. 'I swear some of them have more sizzle that a pan full of rattlesnakes.'

'If you can't stand the heat, Jack, get the hell out of the kitchen!' Munson had a way with words, 'aint that right son.' He turned to shake hands with young Bill Bohl striding towards them.

'It's a pleasure to meet you, Mister Munson.' It was fairly obvious that, despite his experience, he held Bill Munson in the highest regard. Jack introduced the two Bills to each other and the three of them strode towards the stables.

An hour later, with the impressive farm tour over, Jack was sitting behind his desk. Time for business. He offered Bill Munson a drink, and poured them two fingers of Scotch each.

'Thing is, Bill, we only deal in the best here at Black

Watch, you can see that. Our clients demand top quality every time.' Bill looked around at the photos of prize winning cattle on the walls, so Jack continued. 'I got investors beating a path to my door to spend their money. Sure, they might get a better tax advantage in our cattle business, but there's a lotta interest in horses too. For example, the film director, Mike Nichols, you heard of him? Mike was on the phone only yesterday. He has a few cows with us and we share a love of art. I invited him to dinner next week. He loves his horses and out to buy a few for himself. Reckon he's definitely good for a few bucks. And these guys don't mind paying the price. The more they pay, the more they can brag about.'

Bill looked at him sideways. 'What are you trying to sell me, Jack?' A man who had been around horse dealers all his life, he knew a sales pitch when he heard one.

'How 'bout you set me up with some of your best breeding mares, here at Black Watch. My guy will look after them and I can sell them on to my clients as and when.'

The man considered the proposition. 'If I'm hearing you right, you want some of my best breeding stock in your fields, but you don't want to pay me for them? That how it goes?' He pushed his hat back on his head. 'Now why in the hell would I want to do a thing like that?'

Jack was awaiting the question, ready with an answer. 'Because, Bill, these men will pay double what they're worth, hell, even triple if I treat them right.' He looked the man in the eye, as he closed the deal. 'If and when word gets out that your breeding stock is doubling in value, well, that won't do your Shalimar stud no harm, now, will it?'

Heading back out towards the twin engine plane, Bill considered the deal he had just done, and then shook his head. One thing was for sure, that guy sure could sell ice-cream to a dead man!

## Lawyers office, New York - July 1964

'It's your father, Jack.' Jack Dick and Howard Linkwood went back a long way, one of the few men who had stood beside him as a friend as well as business advisor - not that Jack ever took any advice off anybody. He studied the man sitting opposite, in a grey short-sleeved shirt and a club tie he didn't recognise.

'Don't tell me the old bugger has croaked? Do I need a handkerchief?' Jack showed no remorse, almost relief at the thought.

'Far from it, Jack. He is suing you...!'

'He's what?' Jumping up from his chair, Jack's face turned deep red as he shouted out the words.

'Calm down,' the lawyer stayed seated, checking the document in front of him. 'It says that three years ago you signed an agreement with the old man, stating that you would share the profits of your future trading with him.' He looked up, checking his client's reaction, which didn't look good. Before Jack cold protest, he continued. 'It then mentions something about how he paid off your gambling debts and gave you $200 per week for living expenses, when times were hard for you.'

Despite what the lawyer expected, Jack stayed perfectly calm, silenced with his thoughts for a full minute before saying, 'Well, he's a lying bastard.' More silence, before adding, 'what does he want?'

'There's more stuff about your brother, and how they don't have enough money to live on.' The lawyer scanned the rest of the document. 'Says he's sent you letters already but got no reply. Looks like he's looking at compensation. Must have seen the coverage that Black Watch is getting and guessing you are earning enough to get him dealt out and..'

'Is there a copy of the agreement?' Jack butted in.

Linkwood sifted through the papers. 'Here it is. Dated August 16th 1960, with your signature.' He handed it over.

The silence in Howard Linkwood's smart corner office was broken only by the ticking of a glass clock on the wall. The lawyer gazed out of the window over the Manhattan skyline, letting his client do the thinking as he read the document. In the years he had known and worked with Jack Dick, he had learned that, unlike his other clients, it was wise to let the man make his own decisions. Jack was smart, he knew that, but never quite smart enough to keep himself out of hot water. Yes, he was a man of vision about making money and the bigger picture but invariably his dealings from the past came back to haunt him in the present. This was another one of those times and, although to most people it would be a set-back, being sued by your own flesh and blood, he was pretty sure what Jack's next words would be.

'Fuck him!' Jack even let out a smile as he said the words. 'He's just fishing. Not enough in here to hold any more water than a paper hat. Black Watch isn't in my name, so let him see their accounts. He has no access to my private business and let's see it stays that way.' Jack stood up, grabbing his hat from the desk. 'Send him a letter telling him he ain't getting a dime!'

## Black Watch Farms - October 1964

Technically, the 1964 Black Watch Masterpiece sale was the second of its kind, with the inaugural one being held the previous year. However, this time, the whole event had gone up a few gears.

In fact, an invitation to attend the event had become one of the hottest tickets in town. Of course, if you were already an investor in the Black Watch scheme then you assumed automatic inclusion, but it was those who weren't that were being coveted most.

With the company now expanding rapidly, and new farms being leased almost monthly, an invite to a party to surround the sale was essential and Jack made sure that this one would be a party to top all parties.

Special guests had not only been invited from the Angus breeds native Scotland, but plane and travel tickets paid for by the firm. Douneside Farm manager, Vic Findlay, had received his by default, when his boss, Lady MacRobert had declined to represent the bull she had sold. It was Vic's first time to cross the Atlantic and he certainly made the most of it.

Also Tom Todd, the breeder of Escort of Manorhill, made the list, arriving a few days beforehand and getting a guided tour of the farms and their cattle. Another equally distinguished visitor was Roley Fraser, boss of MacDonald-Fraser, the auctioneering firm who ran the famous Perth Bulls sales. Roley was offered the privileged position of guest auctioneer, where he would get to sell a few lots in the sale. In return he would also get to sing the merits of Scottish breeding and justify the top prices that Jack had forked out on clients' behalf for the 'world's' best genetics.

But it wasn't the cattlemen who would be the showpiece of this sale, nor even the cattle themselves, but the celebrity high profile movers and shakers of the front pages. Black Watch now had a long list of investors but still the scheme canvassed more and more to fund the expansion. Doctors, lawyers, dentists and other professionals who sold their services in exchange for extortionate rates, hiding their cash in the tax shelter to protect their pensions, were one thing. But what he really coveted were the people whose names were a household word. It was all about fame as well as fortune. Yes Jack's mind was one hundred percent focussed on business but what an added bonus that he could rub his shoulders against those whom the whole world wanted to be seen with.

There were some, of course, who blankly refused to have their name mentioned, especially men who had earned their fortunes in some of the blacker parts of society. Gangsters, porn kings, charlatans and politicians, a good number of them were keen to exchange their dirty money for something more legitimate. Even for Jack R Dick, a man whose principles could be described as questionable at best, these were not people he wanted his name connected with and would be quite happy to accept payments from a 'front-man' whose real client wished to remain anonymous.

Like all good parties, the Masterpiece Sale spanned a whole weekend, starting on Friday evening with a huge dinner and dance. In the corral where the bulls were normally exercised, two massive green candy-striped marquees were erected, covering the entire area, which had been hired from Barnum Circus.

The 800 guests entered the fray down a long red carpet between flaming braziers, as a string quartet serenaded their arrival. Each guest was met by two concierges, clad in uniform and top hats. They were handed a crystal glass of champagne as they entered.

'Ladies and Gentlemen, Senator and Mrs Al Gore!' a few heads turned as yet another US Senator joined the party.

Jack may have voted for a few democrats over the years but he was never a political man, leaving that to men who liked to gamble their future on the opinion of the masses. No, to him, politicians were a necessary evil but most of them had their uses. In fact, it could well be said, that Jack R Dick had no friends at all, just a great many acquaintances. It would also be said, by most who knew him, that every acquaintance he had would be, in some way or other, useful to him. Oh sure, he would give people the time of day but it never took him long to evaluate of what purpose that conversation would have to his business, be it financial or influential.

'Senator, so glad you could make it,' Jack greeted him off the red carpet. 'This is my wife Lynda.'

The Senator introduced them both to his wife Pauline, leaving the two women to chat while he spoke softly to Jack. 'A heck of a party you got going on here, Jack. Hope it's worth it!'

Dick moved on to the next arriving guest, a good looking fashionable young man in his mid twenties with a super-model of a girlfriend draped on his arm. 'Jack, thanks for the invite. Peter Revson,' he held out his hand.

'Ah yes, our budding young racing driver. I'm told you have a great future on four wheels: World Championship material, they say.' Jack gave him a grin, whispering in his ear. 'Mind you, with a girl like that, I bet it's hard to keep your eyes on the road?' The two men smiled at each other before Jack added. 'Come and see me tomorrow, we should talk a little business.' As with most of his invited guests, Jack had done some research on Revson. Getting into the motor racing sport was an expensive business and, like most other drivers, this was invariably paid for with family money. After a private school education, it would be a playboy lifestyle of yachts in the Caribbean, race horses, wild parties as well as, of course, fast cars. If you were good enough or, more importantly, daring enough, there was always a chance to pit your skills against others on the tarmac until you either ran out of money, or out of road. Peter and his younger brother were nephews of Charles Revson, the mogul who started the hugely successful Revlon cosmetics company. Charles had no children so Peter, as the oldest nephew, was in line to inherit the entire family fortune, estimated at over one billion dollars.

Conversation over, Jack moved on again when he caught sight of his old pal, Steve Lawrence. 'Steve, so good to see you again.' He stepped forward and shook the man's hand. 'And Eydie, you look more gorgeous that ever.' Jack signalled to his wife. 'Lynda, come and say hello to our famous Hollywood couple.' He turned back to Steve. 'Oh, by the way, congratulations on your latest chart success. My wife loves the record. Plays it all the time, don't you darling.' Lynda smiled, greeting the couple.

'Is Connie with you?' she asked.

Eydie shook her head. 'Sorry, she sends her apologies. She has to go to Europe to appear on 'Top of the Pops'.' The Connie in question was Connie Francis, one of America's biggest selling singers during the 1950s. She had been introduced to Jack by Eydie and had paid quite a heavy investment into their scheme.

'Aw shame, I was so looking forward to meeting her,' Lynda replied. The two exchanged small talk for a few minutes while Jack moved on to a couple who were standing at the bar.

'Mister and Mrs E G Marshall,' called out the announcer. Lynda made her excuses with Eydie and went to welcome the latest arrival. 'Mister Marshall, how lovely to meet you.' The man took her hand and kissed it theatrically. 'Or should I call you Lawrence Preston?' Lynda could barely contain herself. 'I just love you in that show, 'The Defenders', you are so, so, clever!'

'Oh that's just an act, Mrs Dick. But the nation seems to like it. Certainly pays the bills.' Marshall was dressed in a dark suit, not dissimilar to the one he wore in the courtroom drama on television.

'Well I preferred him in 12 Angry Men. The strong silent type. Juror number four, wasn't it?' The woman held out her hand, 'Judith Coy, pleased to meet you.' Lynda took the woman's hand. 'I am Everett's wife, well, his latest one anyway.' The woman let out a laugh so loud it turned a few dozen heads around the room.

Jack had wondered outside. Around the sides of the marquee, all of Black Watch's stock bulls had been positioned, each one having their own special wooden pen to lie in, in between bunches of heifers which would be offered for sale. The pens were floodlit, so that revellers could admire them while they wined and dined. And dine they did. If an Aberdeen Angus breeder cannot provide the best beef that money can buy, then it really would be a poor show. He stopped by Evulse, silently watching him with sadness. As if out of nowhere, Gar Douglas appeared at his side, dressed in a smart dinner suit with a black bow tie, rather than his usual denim and Stetson.

'What now, boss?'

Jack pulled in a big sigh. 'End of the road for him, I guess. It was a good story while it lasted.' He turned to Gar. 'See that he goes quietly. Poor old boy has had enough fuss for one life.'

Gar nodded, saying nothing. In the distance, as if to remind the bull of home, the sound of a lone bag-piper could be heard above the noise of the two marquees full of guests. Both men stood silently for a minute, thinking, before Jack patted Gar on the shoulder. 'Come on, right hand man. We're not going to sell any stock standing here. Dinner is waiting.'

As the piper reached the first marquee, a Master of Ceremonies banged a wooden hammer on a solid board. 'Ladies and Gentlemen. Dinner is served!' Following the piper, who was kitted out in kilt and full regalia, were a long line of waiters, all dressed in white, carrying not one but five barons of beef on huge wooden trays at shoulder height, four men to a tray. The piper marched to the centre of the marquee, where a stage had been built, before ending his tune and standing to attention. This was a cue for the crowd to applaud, led by Lynda.

For the next hour, while filling themselves full of Mouton Cadet 1961 and dining on Aberdeen Angus tenderloin the table conversations revolved around beef, both on and off the hoof. A catalogue had been mailed out with every invite for the sale that was due to take place the following evening and many of the assembled breeders compared notes and discussed the merits of certain bulls versus others. Auctioneer, Dave Canning, moved from table to table, answering questions and giving out advice to would-be buyers. A giant of a man, Dave had an almost encyclopaedic knowledge of the breed, and was a well known figure throughout the US. However, this evening was not just about handing out advice but making a mental note of who was interested in which lots, and advising them of a guide price. 24 hours later, that information would be put to great use.

Through the remainder of the evening a modern jazz band wooed the revellers onto the wooden dance floors and carried on way into the early hours. Some of the elder men were encouraged into the main house, where fine brandy and free Cuban cigars helped them relax and get to know the place. Many of them had an idea that Dick was a charlatan who had little real idea about cattle but plenty of idea about business. Like him or not, you had to admire the guy, putting on one of the most lavish parties the breed had ever witnessed. To the older guard, one thing was for sure: with this much money floating around the stockyard, cattle at tomorrow's sale were not going to be cheap.

As with many an entrepreneur, Jack Dick was a man who could manage on very little sleep. Although he and his staff had been liberally handing out the booze, he made sure that he sampled very little of it himself. By 5.30am, he was back at his desk, looking out of the window as daylight rose and the remaining few die-hard party-goers finished up the last few bottles. One or two hadn't made it back to their designated dwellings and he could see a couple of bodies sleeping soundly on some hay bales near the barn. All in all the night had been a great success but it was sale day that was to pay for it. Sure he had spent some money, a lot of money. This party had cost best part of fifty grand. The press had been quick to say that some of Black Watch's bull purchases had been irresponsible and they sure would have something to say about this gig. But today was payback time - it had to be.

Many of the females in the sale were sired by the old stock sire, Elavate of Eastfield who had proved to be a great breeder. 25 of them were to be sold first, offered with breeding privileges to any one of the Black Watch Masterpiece sires that were on display in the yard. Using modern techniques, semen had been taken from all these bulls and stored frozen in tanks in their new storage facility. That was why they were able to offer some of the bulls for sale, including a couple of the Perth Champions themselves. Although they had near milked the bulls dry, nobody would know exactly how much of the frozen stuff they had in store, but it would be enough to keep on using it by artificial insemination on the herd for a few years to come. Just call it insurance.

---

After checking the day's stock markets, something which he did every morning, Jack pulled on his jacket and went down to the yard. An army of farmhands, some drafted in especially for the day, were clearing up empty bottles that had been left over. Others were in with the cattle, washing, brushing and grooming. Jack wandered amongst them offering words of encouragement. Kevin, the young lad who had travelled over with Lindertis Evulse, had a row of bulls tied to a rail and was trimming away at one with a pair of scissors, taking the longer hair off the animals shoulders to make his back look flatter and wider. 'Morning Kevin,' he said quietly. 'They trained you well in Scotland, I see.' The boy glanced up from his work, nodding his appreciation. 'Maybe you can fit me in for a trim later?' Jack let out a light chuckle.

Towards the entrance of the first tent one of the staff was scrubbing at a stone water trough. Jack smiled to himself and spoke to the man. 'Ah yes. The bloody trough, the nation's favorite hang-over cure! Be sure it's right full now. And hand one to every guests you see.' A trough full of Bloody Mary, a lethal cocktail of vodka and tomato juice, had been his wife's idea. It was quite common knowledge that many heavy drinkers started the day with one of these for breakfast, just to take the edge of a thumping headache caused by too much red wine. In Jack's opinion, ladling some of this into a glass and handing it to folks as they arrived back to the yard would be a great way to restart the party again. The last thing he wanted was his potential buyers becoming sober, if he was going to coax their money from the pockets!

The sale itself was to be conducted in the main barn. Although the building had stood for over one hundred years, since Jack took over the farm it had had a major face lift. The outside of the old brick barn had been washed in white paint and then the words Black Watch Farms emblazoned across the outside in 50 foot high lettering that could be seen from the main road and beyond. Inside, cattle pens clung to the outer walls of the building and in the centre a raised platform surrounded by wooden railings had been erected as a purpose-built sale ring with a small booth up above it where the auctioneer would stand. Between the sale ring and the pens, an alleyway about 6 feet across wound its way past the cattle so that buyers and onlookers could view the animals without getting their feet dirty. As an added touch, it was laid in polished marble, something which one of the newspaper reporters that he had shown around the place a few months back had picked up on. 'The cattle at Black Watch Farms live in such luxury that they have a marble-floored barn to sleep in!' Well, if a bit of marble could grab a headline like that, it was worth every penny.

Around the main ring, rows of wooden seating had been erected in a semi circle facing the auctioneer, with polished wooden banisters dividing it up into sections. He had picked up the idea from Perth's antique sale yard, a place where the atmosphere was almost electric. A nice added touch had been to have some cotton cushions made for the ladies to sit on. Each one was stamped with the BW logo.

By 11am some of the prospective buyers were already taking their seats so they could get the best view in the house. The sale wasn't due to start until two o'clock, after a brunch had been served in the marquee. This consisted of a huge spread of smoked salmon, cold sliced beef and a vast array of salads that the very capable caterers had laid on. It also included more alcohol, with champagne, beer and wine freely available.

The alleyways around the cattle were so crowded by late morning that it was near impossible to get a view of the cattle at all and by one o'clock all the seats were taken. Those that couldn't get inside the building stood out back and front and could listen to the sale through loud speakers which relayed the auctioneer's voice across the yard and around the paddocks.

At one thirty prompt, a voice over the tannoy-system, the same one who had introduced the guests the previous evening, silenced the crowd with an announcement. 'Ladies and Gentlemen, the proprietor of Black Watch Farms - Jack R Dick.' To start with just a few ladies clapped their hands together but then the applause gathered pace until it became not just clapping any more but cheers and shouts of a standing ovation that went on for best part of a minute.

'Why, thank you,' Jack oozed, lapping up the attention. 'I hope y'all had a good party?' Again more cheers. 'Welcome to our second Masterpiece sale. Today I believe we have some of the finest cattle in the world on offer.' He glanced down at a few notes on a piece of card in front of him. 'I would like to thank all the team here for presenting the animals in such a great way and especially to Gar Douglas for his incredible cattle skills.' The crowd showed its appreciation until Jack raised his voice above them. 'But I would especially like to thank you, the investors in Black Watch Farms, for making this all happen.'

Dave Canning was next on the microphone, announcing the sale officially open, and introducing the first animal in the sale ring. As expected, the sale trade was brisk with a number of heifers passing the 10,000 dollar mark and one reaching a top of 25,000. After thirty minutes of selling, one of the day's main animals eventually arrived in the ring. This was the Perth Grand Champion of 1964, Escort of Mannorhill. A one third share of this bull was on sale, with the other two thirds being retained by Black Watch.

'Do I hear 75,000 dollars?' Dave spotted a catalogue waving a 'yes' in the front row. From then the bidding jumped in multiples of 10,000 until it reached 150, and then slowed as two bidders battled it out. Eventually, after a full five minutes of coaxing bids out of each of them, the hammer was banged down at 187,500 dollars. At a one third share, this valued the whole bull at 561,000 dollars, by far and away a world record price for any bull. With the bull only costing 7,500 pounds sterling ($12,000) in Perth eighteen months earlier, it didn't take a mathematician to work out that Black Watch Farms was one big profitable organisation, especially when ten minutes later, Essedium of Douneside also sold at 165,000 dollars for a half share.

Total sale proceeds of the day's trading saw 75 head of cattle gross 832,000 dollars, an average of 11,000 each. This trade too set a world record for a single cattle auction in USA.

Top-hat marquees at the 1964 Black Watch sale

Guests dine on finest Scottish beef

## Highway 97, New York - June 1965

Arnold Solomon had heard it all before. Since his days in the military, he had been a chauffeur of some sort or other, driving everyone from Generals to prisoners during his years behind the wheel. He was close to retirement, settling on a small house in Duchess county, quite happy to just grow a few vegetables and tend the garden when his wife had spotted an advert in the local paper for a driver based just a few miles away. A brief interview had demonstrated that he was well qualified for the role which mainly consisted of driving one of the company limousines up state, either to the airport, or to a swanky address in New York. The Black Watch limousine had the letters BW on the side, as did his uniform and peaked cap.

After a few months in the job, he had listened to conversation in the back, mainly about cattle, the price of bull and the tax office. Usually it would be an excited new client who was just buying, or had bought, a herd of top quality cattle and had gotten into the farming business. On more than one occasion he had dropped the passenger off at a fashionable country clothing store on the outskirts of town on the way home, one that knew how to charge folks double just by being nice to them. He had even been invited in by one guy, who was trying on a tweed suit which made him look like something crossed between Sherlock Homes and Robin Hood! Arnold had smiled and said he looked grand and that was just what all wealthy farmers wore these days, which had the desired effect of getting him an extra tip.

But somehow, this guy in the back today was a little different. Arnold knew little about his boss, other than he was a New York city slicker, playing at farming, while making loads of money and making sure folks knew it. He checked the mirror again. The guy he had just collected was young, thin, well dressed, ambitious, and courteous even, much like most of the others. And yet, travelling on his own, he hadn't seemed like the usual punters, who exuded wealth and couldn't wait to spend some of it.

Arnold decided to engage him in conversation, attracting him away from the brochure he was studying. As his eyes met Arnold's in the mirror, the chauffeur felt a shudder running down his spine that made him feel uncomfortable. Recalling his man's name he asked, 'are you considering getting in the cattle business, Mr Madoff?'

'Cattle are not really my thing but word on the street is this guy has a pretty good investment model going on.' Madoff's Jewish accent was quite pronounced and he spoke slowly as though choosing each word personally.

Arnold pressed him a bit further. 'What business are you in just now?'

'I'm in small safe stocks, low risk kind of stuff. Always a good investment. Say, you fancy an investment in a company I know? About to hit the big time any day now. A sure-fire winner!'

Arnold shook his head. 'Wife keeps any spare cash we got up the chimney!' Something in his mind suggested that the boss would need to look out for this one. He certainly didn't seem like the sort who would want to get into farming and tweed clothing, that was for sure.

Soon they pulled off the interstate and his passenger looked out of the window at the dusty fields on the roads leading through Duchess County. The look on his face suggested the countryside wasn't a place he felt comfortable.

## Wappingers Falls Ranch - August 1965

Black cattle in the paddocks around the ranch scattered as the thud-thud of rotors buzzed overhead, running in all directions. Below them, clouds of brown dust swirled up into the sky, almost blocking out the pilot's vision as the Bell Jet-ranger helicopter turned in a circle, lowering itself to the ground. Jack shouted out to the pilot from the passenger's seat for him to 'wait there' as the rotors started to slow down and he opened the door. Covering his mouth with his hands and squinting with his eyes, he climbed out of the machine and ran through the dust across the gravel yard towards a waiting group of people. As he neared, he shouted out, above the noise of the engine which was now running at half throttle. The shout was to Gar Douglas. 'Come on, we're going for a ride! Bring Patti.'

Gar could barely hear what the boss was saying but his wife Patti heard it clear enough and tugged him by the arm, a big grin on her face. In all her life she had wanted a trip in a helicopter and she hadn't needed asking twice. Holding tightly on to his leather hat, Gar followed Jack back to the machine, noticing the emblem on the door saying BW. Jack opened the rear door and climbed in, beckoning Patti to take the front seat and Gar to join him in the back. Making sure the doors were securely closed he signalled to the pilot who accelerated the engine again. With the door shut, Gar pulled his hat back on and looked across to his boss.

'We bought a helicopter?' he asked in a loud voice.

'Bell 206 Jet-ranger,' he recited above the noise. 'Twin engines, built for the military. Safest thing in the sky!'

Within seconds the aircraft rose vertically and then tilted forward like a ride at the funfair. The ground dropped away from them and Patti was waving down from the front with one hand, holding on to the seat with the other. Her children, now tiny figures in the dust below, were waving back.

Gar pointed to the animals in the field, which were running again, leaving a trail of dust behind them.

'It spooks the cows a bit, but they'll get used to it.' Jack grinned to his right hand man. 'This is the future of travel. It can get us to Fishkill Plains in about four minutes.' Already the familiar sight of the barn and paddocks of the ranch were behind them out of sight, as the chopper gathered speed to near 100 miles per hour. 'Now we have taken leases on farms further afield, this will save a lot of time and effort for both you and me.' Jack stopped and the two men took in the view of the fields below, littered with cattle appearing as little black dots. 'By the way, we're going to need some more cows. I took on a new investor and he is keen to take a big slice. A young hotshot, name of Madoff. Putting in best part of a hundred grand. I dropped the price to him from 4,500 each to 3,500 dollars to get the deal. So, you can go shopping again, Gar. No need to get the best if he's not paying top dollar though. The kid wouldn't know an angus from an anus!'

Shortly the buildings on the Fishkill ranch came into view and Gar could make out the newly built calving facilities. From now on, all the cows in this area would be brought to this one place to have their calves, where they could be monitored by just a couple of men. The cattle sheds even had closed circuit TV cameras situated throughout, so night activity could be monitored from one office. Since the computer system had got up and running, information on each cow could be displayed on a tiny green screen in the same office, with a little help from a technical guy. Gar hadn't got wholly to grips with it yet but, along with travelling through the sky, it certainly did feel like the company was well ahead of its time compared to some of the other farmers in the area. That was Jack's way, not only making the place more efficient, but getting one over on what he always referred to as the 'ma and pa' operations of yesteryear. The new technology also helped bring in the investors too, when he and some of the sales guys could bamboozle them with statements about calving mass, recessive characteristics and favourable rates of depreciation! Even Gar had no idea what they were talking about but it sounded impressive and that's what mattered.

The chopper circled the farm buildings once and then levelled up and landed in a small paddock. Jack opened the door and climbed out, shouting to Patti in the front. 'You guys go on back and take the kids a ride up!'

As the machine kicked up the dust again, Jack headed over to a car that was parked in the yard. A haggard looking man in a v-necked jersey and receding hairline leant against the fence, smoking a cigarette which he stubbed out under one foot as Jack reached him. 'Earl, sorry to keep you. Jack Dick. Welcome to Black Watch Farms.' Jack held out his hand.

'That was some entrance, Mister Dick!'

Earl Wilson was old school and Jack knew he would take some impressing, which is why he planned his little stunt. But he was also a big hitter, not just in New York, but as a national journalist who had also been in a few films. Much of his writings revolved around the gossip columns, the sort of stuff that Jack's mother used to read, and he had a way of making things interesting, even if they weren't. More recently he had made the headlines publishing a book about the extra-marital affairs of the recently deceased President Kennedy which had raised a few eyebrows in the senate. Already he had pulled out a notebook, scribbling something down before asking, ' you travel like that all the time?'

'We are cutting edge here at Black Watch, Earl, embracing anything that helps us be more efficient.' He omitted to mention that he had only bought the helicopter that very day, as he headed towards the new office building, Wilson trailing behind him. 'We are not quite the stereotype farmer that you see in cowboy films, Earl.'

'You certainly aren't, Mister Dick,' he mumbled.

Jack ignored him, ushering him into the office and then letting him take in the space for himself. The building had a low ceiling layered with white plastic tiles, and a line of desks were studded with various machines including a typewriter and some screens, one of which was making a whirring sound. A secretary looked up as they entered and he asked her to fetch some coffee, raising a questioning eyebrow at the reporter. Earl nodded, making a show of looking out of the window and adding, 'don't tell me you got a McDonald's round the back as well?' He winked at the secretary.

Jack gave him a look that suggested 'I tell the jokes round here,' and then took a seat in front of the computer terminal, punching a few buttons on the keyboard. A green screen glowed with a list of bull sales this month, just as the man stood behind him. 'As you can see, Earl. We are not just a 'ma and pa' operation.' Earl was writing a couple of figures in his notebook before Jack killed the screen again and spun around in his chair. Earl turned his eyes to the TV screen instead which showed a long shed full of cows all lying down chewing their cud. The picture rotated to another one, every thirty seconds. 'Maternity ward,' Jack offered.

Over the next few minutes Jack answered some questions, while the man drank his coffee, before bundling him into the seat of a Cadillac parked out front, and taking him on a tour of the estate. They finished up at

Wappingers Falls ranch, driving up past the massive sculpture of a black bull in the entrance, just as a line of real bulls were getting a wash and brush up in the yard.'

The reporter looked along the line, scratching his head. 'Mister Dick,' he mused. 'In my trade, I have visited a lot of beauty salons in my time but that sure is a lot of bull!'

## Sotheby's, London - September 1965

'Richard, good to meet you, buddy.'

Richard Brown, an established well known London art dealer, eyed up Jack Dick in a moment's silence before shaking his hand. Dick's reputation arrived well before he did, when he had announced his intentions in the art world by picking off a couple of pieces by James Seymour the previous year from under their noses. Another loud mouthed Yank who was definitely not his buddy. He had seen them come and go, throwing their weight around and making lucky purchases. Sporting art was Brown's domain, which was why Jack had set up the meeting.

'What can I do for you?' Richard answered curtly, after the two of them sat down with a coffee.

Jack smiled at the arrogance of the man. Dealers were all the same the world over, he of all people should know that. Whether it was art, cattle, guns, stocks or real-estate, the game is always played by people, with people! But the key ingredient was knowledge, and in this game, that was something Jack was learning very fast. He ran his hand over his forehead, taking a deep breath. 'Way I see it, it is what I can do for you, Richard. You see, I got a passion for this sort of art.' He glanced around the gallery, walls adorned with 18th century paintings of horses. 'And I got money. Lots of money.' Richard went to butt in but Jack raised his hand. 'I know, I know. You have plenty of clients with money, right. All of them limeys, I guess. So you don't want me as a client as well?' He could see in the man's eyes that he had hit a nerve so he added a greasy smile to rub in the salt. 'Wrong, Richard. You DO want me as a client, and I'll tell you why. You wanna know why?' Jack's eyes bored into the man in his spotted bow-tie and

English upper-class manner. 'Because you don't want me as an enemy, Richard!' The smile was a grin now. 'I make a really, really bad enemy. Do you understand?'

Coming from some people, this could have been constituted as a threat but somehow, coming from Jack Dick, it seemed a lot more friendly, as though the man had just offered him some sort of treaty. Richard took his time to answer. 'What exactly is it you are looking for?'

Jack stood up, scraping his chair back on the mosaic tiled floor. 'I am a fair man, most folk will tell you that. So, Richard, what I am looking for is that we share some stuff. You know. Like kids do with candy. One for you, one for me. That kinda thing?' Richard said nothing, so he added. 'That way, nobody gets their fingers burnt?'

'How will I know when you're bidding? Which ones you are after? Who will be bidding for you?' It was a simple question.

'Oh, you'll work it out, Dickie, old boy. You'll work it out.' With that Jack sauntered out of the high ceilinged room, mission accomplished, leaving the man somewhat confused. This was the third art dealer he had met with that morning, saying the same to each. His plan was to periodically use one or other of them to buy on his behalf, so they all got a commission out of it, keeping each one on side. But, to keep them on their toes and, more importantly off his back, he would put out rumours on certain paintings that he had another dealer doing his bidding, naming a fictitious value, and then watch them bid against each other, driving the price up. Compared to the stock market, this art game was easy pickings, or so it appeared.

Later that morning, Jack sat down with sporting art specialist, Brian Watson, to find out that, in his case anyway, it just got a little harder.

'I did warn you, Jack.' Watson was immaculately

dressed in a grey suit and red tie. 'I am based mainly in New York these days but I had to be here for this meeting today. It was almost like it was my fault. The powers-that-be are trying to stamp down on their precious art leaving the country. A meeting of the British Museum directors have explored the ancient laws and come up with some crazy notion in the National Treasures Act that many years ago the King, god knows which one, sanctioned a law that says if anyone outwith Great Britain buys a piece of work that they think should stay in the country, they will be allowed to commandeer it, paying the exact sale price.'

'That's ridiculous,' was Jack's first reaction. He thought for a minute. 'Is this aimed directly at me? I am flattered.'

'Your name was mentioned, yes. Along with Mellon.'

'Damn that Mellon. He is always in my way!' Paul Mellon was heir to the Mellon Banking dynasty, started by his grandfather in Pittsburgh nearly one hundred years back. It was well documented that the Mellon boys were some of the richest guys in US, collectively worth a few billion dollars. They had donated so much money to the National Gallery in Washington that the place had an entire wing named after them. Paul had similar interests in 18th century art as Dick.

'There were a few others in there as well. You guys have got them riled!'

Jack looked at Brian for a minute, thinking. 'Reckon there might be a way of making money in that somewhere. What say I buy a picture privately for fifty grand, and get an invoice for, say, one hundred. That would show the bastards!'

Brian raised his eyes to the chandelier above his head. 'I'll pretend I didn't hear that,' he replied, shaking his head. He stood to leave. 'I am just warning you Jack. Be careful, OK?' He placed his hand on the man's shoulder. As usual, Jack wasn't listening as he ran a few scenarios through his mind.

### Staunton, Virginia - October 1965

Dave Canning was a big man in many ways. Six foot six in stature, it was his knowledge of the cattle industry that put him up there with the Leachmans and a few others. Originally from the Red River Valley in New Mexico, Canning had made his way east to Virginia as a boy, working with black cattle in King William County before setting up on his own in the foothills of Shenandoah Valley near Staunton. Using a philosophy he had learned back home, Canning's outlook on Angus cattle was different to others around that time, where he advocated that the breed were bred to stand the mountains of Scotland and hence should spend their time outside. His farm in Staunton extended to over 8,000 acres, much of which was hill and forestry land.

An association with Black Watch had firstly come through Leachman but then, unlike Leachman who fell out of favour with Jack Dick soon after, Canning hung around and got involved in the business. Gar Douglas had a lot of time for Canning and valued his experience. For Jack, however, it wasn't so much his experience but his contacts within the cattle world that were more of interest. For all Black Watch had nearly one hundred investors now, it needed credibility in real Angus breeders, those with a track record of running their own herds instead of having them 'managed'.

For their first Masterpiece sale in 1963, it had been Dave Canning who had done much of the organising for Black Watch, bringing in genuine clients and talking up the cattle. Like any good salesman, he was not adverse to doubling or trebling the price if he thought the punter could afford it. To the contrary, the more they paid, to the untrained eye, the better product they considered they had. Dave had worked closely with Garfield Douglas too, especially when the outfit had started to expand beyond its own boundaries in Duchess County. He had been instrumental in bringing in other cattle farmers, persuading them to sell their own herds and then lease the farm back to Black Watch, managing Angus cattle on their behalf. By 1965, the outfit was now running a couple of thousand head, on nearly a dozen farms, when he eventually succumbed to leasing part of his own place in Virginia to the company. A month or two later, a Black Watch investor visited him on his Sugar Loaf Farm in his shiny Cadillac, hoping to get a look at a new cow he had just invested a lot of money in. A doctor from Lawrenceville, Brunswick county, he had expected to see the animal in its own comfortable wooden pen, bedded in deep straw with a trough full of grain to eat, as they had been in New York. Much to his disappointment, he left after being told that the animal was 'somewhere up there in the timber' and if he wanted to get a look at it the only way up was on horseback!

It was later that year, as a keen-eyed breeder, Canning started to discover more and more discrepancies in the data that he was being fed from the Black Watch offices, something which rang alarm bells in his mind, not only about the capabilities of the whole operation, but their integrity as well. When a list showing he had an animal in the herd with ID number 18 was scrutinised and found to be incorrect, Jack Dick dismissed it with a flick of the wrist, commenting that they were 'all just cattle Dave, get over it'.

It wasn't until October that he started making a few checks of his own, getting Jenny Stevens, a pretty young girl who worked on the data punch system, to run some records through the computer at Fishkill Plains Ranch when no one was around. Scribbling down a few notes, he took numbers of animals and their written down values, verses what had actually been paid for them, and it was pretty evident that the gap was widening. Whereas in the early days, top quality cattle had been purchased, now the standard of stock was falling way below expectations. Moreover, another issue he uncovered was the calving percentages. Black Watch told its customers that the herd was averaging 85-90% (85-90 calves per hundred cows) when in reality, this was nearer 45-50%.

It didn't take a smart mathematician, let alone an experienced cattle breeder, to estimate that if this trend continued, somewhere along the line, things wouldn't add up.

On October 14th, three days before the annual Masterpiece sale, Dave Canning met Jack and Gar in Jack's office, raising his concerns. At first Jack denied all knowledge of it, stating that Canning must have his facts wrong. Gar remained silent, looking mainly at his boots. A heated discussion evolved, during which Dave Canning left the office, slamming the door so hard it near came from its hinges.

The following day a telegram arrived saying that Dave Canning from Staunton, Virginia resigned from all activities to do with Black Watch Farms, and that their cattle residing on his premises were to be removed immediately.

The sale prices in the 1965 event never reached the heights of the previous year, partly due to Canning's non-involvement. Jack announced to all that he was disappointed in the way that Canning had looked after the cattle on his ranch, and that he had fired him as a result. Later Jack was to accuse Dave Canning of trying to sabotage his operation.

## Wappingers Falls - 1966

'There's someone here to see you, Mister Dick.' Jack glanced up at his secretary and nodded his head. He had seen the car pulling up the drive and recognised the Florida plates. Over the last few months he had been half-expecting this visit, glancing out of the window at two men and a woman getting out of the vehicle and strolling towards the front door. He could hear his wife Lynda opening the door and speaking to them, and then his two children.

'You must be Lori,' said the woman. 'My how you've grown.' By the time Jack reached the main hallway of the house, she was talking to Johnny. 'How old are you now, Jonathan?'

'That's not really any of your business,' Jack said harshly.

It was the old man who spoke to him first. 'Jack, how are you?'

Jack's eyes narrowed. 'What are you doing here, Dad?'

'When you didn't reply to my letters, I thought we better come check you were OK.' He looked his son up and down. 'At least say hello to your Mom and your brother?'

Jack gave his mother a brief kiss on the cheek and then shook Elliot's hand without looking him in the eye. Lynda was inviting them through to the living room, offering some tea. 'They're not staying,' Jack interrupted. His wife gave him a glare but he wasn't interested, just standing in the doorway, arms folded.

'We just thought it would be nice to see you, son.' His mother's voice seemed frail since the last time they had spoken. 'It's been nearly five years.' She gave him a smile that only a mother can give a child.

'Well, you've seen me,' he sniffed. 'And now, if you'll excuse me, I have work to do.' With that he turned on his heel and headed back towards his office.

Making excuses for him, Lynda followed and caught him by the arm at the bottom of the stairs. 'Jack!' her eyes looked fierce. 'They have come all this way, Jack. Your own parents and your brother. Come near a thousand miles to see you.'

'No they haven't come to see me. They're here for my money. Just like always!'

'That's not fair Jack. At least let them stay a while. They hardly even recognise their own grandchildren.' She let go of his arm as he turned to her.

'Not fair?' Jack rarely raised his voice to anyone, let alone his wife. 'Not fair? You sound just like them. Not fair that some folk work hard and make money while others do nothing and expect folks to hand it to them. Not fair that my brother has no job and my Dad sits around all day blaming everyone and everything for his own troubles.' He looked over Lynda's shoulder at his father standing in the doorway behind and thought how frail he looked. 'You wanna know what's not fair? Life. That's what.'

Lynda turned away, close to tears, and her father-in-law gave her a hug. 'Let me talk to him,' he said softly. 'Just for a minute. You go and see Betty. She's been wanting to make this trip for a long time.'

'He won't see reason, Sam,' Lynda dabbed at her eyes with a white handkerchief. 'You know what he's like?' The two smiled at each other then she headed back to the living room, leaving him standing alone. Sam Dick looked up at the ornate staircase, taking in the splendour of the décor and took a deep breath before heading upwards. At the top of the stairs he saw an office away to his left and headed along the corridor, smiling at a secretary sitting at a polished desk. Before she had chance to buzz through on the intercom, Sam was past her and opening the office door marked up with Jack R Dick. Inside, his son was sitting behind a large carved wooden desk, waiting for him. The two men locked eyes before Jack indicated for him to sit down.

Both stayed silent for best part of a minute, Sam glancing around the room at prints of black bulls posing for photos in front of smiling people he didn't recognise.

Eventually it was Jack who broke the silence. 'So, how have you been?'

'Gotta tell ya, Jack. It's not been easy,' Sam's Brooklyn accent was much more pronounced than his son's, despite that he now lived down in Florida. He got straight to the point. 'Those investments, Jack. That agreement. I thought we had a deal?'

'A deal. Sure, we had a deal. I've been sending money, haven't I? After your last demand.' Jack's eyes were narrowing, the brief, guilty compassion evaporating as quick as it came. 'You sued me, you bastard. Did you really think that was going to work? Bullying me into giving you money!'

Sam visually retreated a little, trying to stay calm. 'You wouldn't return my letters, Jack. What else was I to do?'

Jack considered this, which was partly true. Since his lawyer had read out the lawsuit two years previous, it was his wife Lynda who persuaded him to relent. Of course Jack had made a deal with the man. But Jack had made a lot of deals, in the past. And that is exactly where they stayed. The past was the past. And the future was where the answers lay. Why couldn't anyone else see that?

Everyone has charge of their own course. *Develop success from failure*, that's what Dale Carnegie had said, wasn't it? That is exactly what he had done. Those dark years were behind him and what happened back then stayed there; their only possible use was to be a springboard into the success of the future. What he had now: a sound business, some would call a big business, most would see a successful business; that was his and his alone. Not his father's or his family's. Not owned by the past, not even attributed to it. It wasn't that he didn't like his father, or wanted to spite him in any harmful way; just that he didn't owe him. Not on any sort of scale, despite what they might have agreed back then. Over the last year and a half he had been sending money into the man's account, just a few thousand a month, but enough to live on. As much as he deserved, possibly more.

He looked at the man sitting opposite, his hair line so far receded, the rest of it snow white. How old was he, 62, 63? Jack couldn't even remember. 'I sent you money, ' he said again, quietly. 'What more do you want?'

Sam took in a deep breath and said what he came to say. 'This Jack. This is what you promised me and your brother.' He looked around the walls again, and out of the window. 'You said if I could give you a leg-up, get your life back on track, one day you would make it big, and then we could share it out. An investment in all our futures, you termed it.'

Jack bit hard into his lip, drawing on Carnegie for the second time in a few minutes. *Fighting will never get you enough, yielding will get you more.* Eventually he stood up and held out his hand for the man to shake. 'Of course, Dad.' He smiled. 'Let's do this together. I'll get my guys to work out another agreement and make sure you get what you deserve.'

Sam looked at him quizzically. 'Really?'

Jack nodded. 'Thanks for coming up to see us, Dad.'

He was already showing the man to towards the door. 'Now, if you will excuse me, I do really have a couple of urgent things to get done here.' As the door closed behind him he reached into a draw under the desk and pulled out a copy of the agreement that he had signed all those years ago, glanced at it and smiled. Then he screwed it up and threw it at the door. 'You'll get just what you deserve!'

## Las Vegas - September 1966

'What the business needs is more headlines.' Jack looked around at the Vice Presidents sitting at the table, his assembled generals. As well as Douglas there was Bill Ragals, a hotshot New York attorney and the man he had appointed as Head of Development. Next to him Joe Moretti, an accountant not only with the highest credentials but with the most creative mind he had met when it came to figures. Apart from himself that was. Between them, these two men had a close handle on the dealings within Black Watch Farms and, in Joe's case, his own personal goings on. Gar was more a cattleman, not that he was stupid, but it wasn't in his own interest to be privy to Jack's personal accounts. No, when it came to anything other than cattle, Gar was informed on a need to know basis.

'Well if you want to make a splash, Vegas sure is the place to be. What else did you have in mind?' This was Ragals.

Joe Moretti got to his feet. 'Problem as I see it, we need to bring in at least another dozen investors soon. Guys with big money. This operation is expanding so fast, we can't keep up. And we can't sell the cattle, not on the open market.'

All four of them knew the reason for this. Now running over 20,000 head, the cows were churning out 4-5000 calves per year and there just wasn't the market for this number of cattle for breeding in US. They were already putting about 20% of them to the abattoir but the returns were at a fraction of what they were worth, or perceived to be worth, as breeding bulls as cows. This was having an impact on the bottom line which is why Joe had gone to Jack expressing that they needed to do something. Gone were the days that, whenever the sales guys snared another investor, Gar would go out and buy some stock females. Now, the females were all sourced within the herd. If a new guy came along and wanted to buy give cows - the entry level requirement into the scheme - he was expected to pay 3,500 dollars each for them, the new reduced price. These animals would then be bought from the herd of one of the other investors, less Black Watch's commission, thus maintaining the value of their breeding stock.

On paper, Black Watch Farms still looked like a highly profitable and growing business. Of the cattle they were now running, at least a couple of thousand of them were owned by the firm. The remainder were the property of their eighty investors, or partners, as they were known. Most of these were run on leased farms, numbering 50 different sites across a dozen or more states in US. Income revenue streams came from charging the investors a management fee for each animal, plus taking a commission on the cost of their feed amounting to approximately $350 a year per head. There were also other commissions, such as one from the farmers leasing their land to the company. Although some investors had paid cash directly for their investments, others had bought into the scheme in installments. For example, a doctor from Illinois, had pledged $50,000 to buy 10 animals that would be managed and fed over a five year period, and he would pay that in cash payments on a fifty two month instalment plan, charged at 7.5% interest. As this was a written down contract, the full value of these forward leases were written down in the company books as assets.

'What we can't do is let our investors know the real value of our stock,' Regals said. 'If we do that, some of these guys might be smart enough to want to pull their money, but more importantly, some of them might stop making the payments.'

Jack sat quietly, listening to his vice president and then banged his hand flat on the table. 'For god's sake, Bill. Quit telling us what not to do and tell us what we can do!'

Bill looked nervous at the outburst. 'Well, this event should gather more interest from the West. Our salesmen in the East have upped their game since we increased their commissions. As long as we can pull in upwards of ten new investors, we should be in the clear.'

Jack nodded slowly and then looked to Joe inquisitively.

'The receipts from the butchers can get lost in the system for a while, so we can hold on to the value of the cattle and keep the books looking attractive.' Moretti, a plump man in his mid thirties was more than capable of losing information if required. Over the last year, he and Jack had set up Black Watch Farms Inc, a subsidiary of Black Watch Farms, and a limited company which listed all its investors as shareholders, running a whole new set of accounts. The original Black Watch Farms had been a partnership in which Jack owned 50%, the rest divided up between Richard Terker, his brother in law, and small percentages by his VPs and couple of other investors. The lines between the two companies were blurred enough that it was virtually impossible to trace transactions between them.

'Before we lose them, can you drop them by my office next week, Joe?' Jack had ideas about how he could settle that one. It was surprising what you could do with a Tippex pen and a few extra zeros in the right column! Finally he looked across at his number two, who had been sitting quietly taking it all in. 'Anything to add, Gar?'

Although looking a little nervous, Gar was always a man to speak his mind. 'We are needing some more bulls, Jack. They got foot and mouth disease in Scotland, so we can't spend money over there to raise the profile. And we sold a share in most of the ones we bought. Just now we are running a plan to use some of our home-bred bulls in the herds but the gene-pool is tightening...'

'Got any good news, Gar? Bill asked.

'Sure. To start with it finds us a new internal market for our bulls. Some of the best cattle in the world are inbreds! Some of the folks too! Look at the British Royal family, hell, everyone is everyone else's cousin over there, and they do alright!' This raised a smile from the other men. 'Jim Lingle over at Wye has been running experiments of putting half-brother bulls back through the herd and getting some good results.'

Jack spoke next. 'So let me get this straight. We are going to announce that very soon this herd is going to be as inbred as the rednecks hicks down in the deep south?'

Gar stared him down. 'No Jack, we are going to announce a brand new concept of cattle breeding, after being proven by the Wye Valley College under one of the world's leading scientists. We call it line breeding, with reinstated homogeneity!'

Jack raised a grin. 'Hell, Gar, you ever thought of getting into marketing!' He stood to his feet. 'OK fellas, let's get this show on the road!'

The show in question was another of Black Watch's latest marketing events. No longer content with drawing in folks once per year to their Masterpiece sale, a series of extravaganzas had been organised throughout the US to woo new clients. And the one in Vegas would be the daddy of them all. Anyone who was anyone, the more high profile the better, was invited along to the spectacular show which would pull out all the stops. Dancing girls, big bands and modern musical displays would be preceded by a dinner and what better to give a bunch of would-be cattle investors than a dinner of Aberdeen Angus steak, which would certainly help Joe Moretti's accounts!

Once dinner was over, Jack made a poignant speech about the way the government was torturing the little man, trying to pull in high taxes. He had to choose his words carefully as there were at least four senators present. The room was also full of high-rollers, many of them already tanked up on too much drink, who were always up for a good party. Jack and at least a dozen of his salesmen worked the room, using those they knew to introduce them to new faces and possible investors.

At the pinnacle of the party, a large white cake was rolled in to the centre of the room and placed near Jack's table. The cake featured a model of an Angus bull on the top and was to represent Black Watch's fourth birthday, since they had bought the farm and started the scheme with a few cows. Once a line of reporters were suitably arranged, Jack went to cut the cake but as he did so, the top burst open and a very beautiful girl wearing pretty much nothing appeared from it, covered in icing and cream. It certainly was as spectacle and one which had the desired effect, setting off flashbulbs two to the dozen.

## Federal Bank, Wappingers Falls - Feb 1967

'Bob. How you doing today,' Jack smiled at the young cashier. 'Like the tie. You sure do dress snappy. Say, did they give you a raise yet. I put in a good word for you with the boss last week.'

The assistant bristled, grinning from ear to ear. 'Thank you, Mister Dick.'

'Yeah, they oughta listen to me, I am this bank's biggest customer.'

'You sure are, Sir. Now what can I do for you today?'

Jack laid a bankers check on the counter. 'See this, it was made out to a supplier of mine.' The guy nodded. 'But I played golf with him last week and, guess what? He said he would rather take the payment in cash. Says he won't get chance to get to the bank and cash it himself, and he needs the cash to pay for some doctors treatment for his old Mom.'

Bob looked nervously at the check made out to Dixie Farms, for $8,000. 'I'm not sure I am allowed to cash checks paid to folks other than yourself, Mister Dick.'

Jack gave him a winning smile. 'Sure you are Bob, banks do it all the time.' He patted the man's arm. 'You can do that for me, surely. I am the bank's biggest customer. Wouldn't want to upset me now, would you, so I took by business elsewhere? I'm not sure that would get you a raise, would it Bob?'

The man relented, glancing around before opening the cash drawer. 'Tens, or twenties?'

'Twenties will be fine, Bob, thank you.' Folding the cash into his pocket, he smiled again. 'Nice doing business with you. You have a great day now, you hear?'

What the bank failed to know was that Gar had bought eight cows from Dixie Farms, Georgia, for 750 bucks each. Jack had taken the invoice into his office and, at 5am when the place was quiet, made a copy of it, adding a one in front of the figure. This invoice would go through the Black Watch accounts saying eight cows cost $1750 each. Two checks were written to cover the amount, one for $6000 which was sent directly to the supplier and the other, well, it would be pretty much untraceable. Jack whistled a happy tune to himself as he stepped out into the street.

## Art Gallery, Soho, London - December 1966

For a few seconds, Richard Brown glanced around the walls at the daubs and splodges of paint on white canvasses, with a couple of seascapes thrown in, depicting bathers against a purple sky. Then he looked back down at the gilt-framed picture resting on the floor, no longer worthy of its display position.

'OK, five thousand it is.' Brown shook hands with the older man in his corduroy jacket and cravat. All these so called fashionable London galleries were giving way to the modern era, which suited him just fine.

Within minutes, Richard was on the telephone to New York in a phone box in Piccadilly square. 'Hello, Jack.' He had to shout above the noise of the traffic in the busy central London street. I got the Munnings for five grand. The guy wanted eight but I knocked him down. I think it will go up in value. Alfred Munnings' work is very underrated. It's the way he uses pastel colours instead of sharp outlines, not everyone's cup of tea.' Brown listened to his client. 'What's that? Another invoice?'

'You heard me, Richard,' came the voice down the phone. 'We don't need everyone to know our business do we. So you buy the painting on your account. And then resell it to me for one thousand.'

'Are you mad?' Richard nearly spat out his tongue. 'Sell it to you for a loss.'

He listened some more. 'Oh, I'll pay you the full price Richard. And a two hundred pound bonus on top. You put the Munnings through your books at say eight hundred, then write me an invoice for a grand. I'll wire the money today. The other four will find its way to your personal account, Richard. You do have one of those, don't you? Mine is in Switzerland. Great people, the Swiss. Make excellent watches, you know.'

'Watches!' Richard was shouting again. 'Watches, what have watches got to do with anything.' When he listened again, the phone line had gone dead.

## Wappingers Falls Ranch - July 1967

'You'll get your money,' Jack had avoided taking this phone call at least three times, 'my guys are on it right now. I know it's a couple of months overdue, we had a few problems calving those cows, Sir. Client wasn't happy the way they had been looked after and just withheld a couple of payments, that's all. It'll be sorted next week, I swear.' He ran his hand through his hair. 'And the same to you, Sir.'

Joe Moretti sat across the desk from him, shifting uncomfortably in his chair. 'I can't keep them off your back for long, Jack. These farmer guys are pretty easy going but they're gonna need paying sooner or later.'

'I know, I know, Joe. Can we get another loan?'

'Not if it gets out that we owe a year's payment to 50 angry farmers, we can't!' Joe was staying calm but it had been getting harder and harder to make the figures stack up. Jack stayed silent, waiting for the answer. Joe nodded his head, letting out a sigh. 'Sure, on paper we still look good. I reckon we could cover the payments, it's just...'

Jack looked across at him and he looked away.

'Just what, Joe. Spit it out?'

Joe took a deep breath. "Well the regular banks don't like lending to us any more Jack. They are saying cattle is a risky business. So we are having to use, er, other finance companies. And they don't mind, but it's the interest, Jack. We are looking at twenty percent. Twenty five, maybe.'

Jack looked completely un-phased by the news.

'Just get the money, Joe.' He didn't look up this time, still focussing on a newspaper back page, checking the racing results. 'You let me worry how we pay it back. Oh, and another thing. Let's not put it in the headlines, eh? Nobody needs to know who, where or why we borrow money.'

Joe was still fidgeting in his chair, saying nothing, but wanting to. Jack looked him directly in the eye. 'Come on, out with it. Say your piece.'

Joe let out his breath. 'I just think we are getting in too deep, Jack. I can only work the figures for so long before somebody starts to take a look at us.'

Jack nodded slowly. 'The Commission, you think? Nah, they aren't bothered with cattle dealers like us, Joe.' Jack thought back to how the Securities Exchange Commission had looked into his dealings in the past but was pretty confident that that would be a long way off yet.

'There is another way, Jack.' Joe blurted out his next statement, as though it was trying to burst his insides. 'We could always sell?'

## Christies auctions, London - December 1966

'Excuse me, Mister Rolland could you step this way please?'

Peter Rolland span round to face a man wearing a grey suit and half round glasses. 'What's this about?'

'This way, if you don't mind, Sir,' the man repeated. The art dealer found himself in a small room leading off the main gallery, where another man waited for him. With an air of the old guard about him, the man didn't take long in coming to the point.

'Mister Rolland, this afternoon you purchased two works, one by the artist Jon Nost Sartorius for 11,000 guineas, the other by Henry Alken senior, 'The Belvoir Hunt', for considerably more.' The man took his glasses off to clean them before referring to the paper in front of him again. 'Can you tell me what you intend to do with them, Mister Rolland?'

Rolland, a young and enthusiastic art dealer was more into modern art that this older stuff but a commission was a commission. 'Hang them in my lavatory,' he said, his tone cocky cockney.

The man ignored him. 'I am assured that a) you do not have the funds to buy such works for pleasure and b) this is not your style of art at all.'

'Who's asking?' Rolland was still not sure what this was about.

'My name is Henderson, I work for the British government.' He let out a sigh, 'now can we please be a bit more cooperative, Mister Rolland? You have exactly one minute to divulge who commissioned you to buy these paintings, or you will accompany me to Scotland Yard?'

Rolland changed his tune when he heard those words. 'Scotland Yard? What's it got to do with them?' The man just tapped his foot, waiting for an answer. It didn't take long for the dealer to consider the situation; no one wanted Scotland Yard prying about into their affairs. Some of the pictures that had come through his gallery were, not to put too fine a point on it, from a dodgy source. But this one was genuine. A nice little afternoon's work to make a few quid. 'Some bloke from New York. Phoned me yesterday. Told me exactly which two 'e wanted me to buy and said the money would be wired through immediately.'

'A name, if you would be so kind?'

'Dick. Name was Dick, from Greenwich.'

Henderson smiled and sat down, looking at a piece of paper again. 'Well, Mister Rolland,' he said, eventually, looking up above the glasses. 'I have a requisition here from the British Museum. Signed by the Chancellor himself, as it happens. Would you like to see it?' he waved the paper in front of the man and then whipped it away again. 'It seems that the Museum would also like these two paintings.'

'Not for sale,' Rolland muttered, nervously shifting from one foot to the other.

'Maybe you misunderstood me. They have no intention of buying them from you, Mister Rolland. They are going to take them off your hands for exactly the same price that you bid for them.' Henderson stared the man down, and then shook his head. 'The Museum would like to put them in their gallery so the British public can view them. For a small fee of course.'

Rolland was protesting. 'What about my fee, and what about my client?'

'Your client is an ignorant Yank, Mister Rolland. We

don't want our finest treasures getting into his grubby hands do we, to be hung in some vulgar replica mansion and leered at by fat bankers?' For the first time, Henderson was smiling. 'And as for your fee, well you would have to take that up with your client.' He produced another document and laid it on the table, unscrewing the lid off a fountain pen. 'Sign here, please Mister Rolland.'

The dealer made to protest some more and then remembered the words Scotland Yard, and bent over, signing where indicated.

'Thank you, Mister Rolland.' Henderson said smugly. 'Don't let me detain you any longer!'

An hour later, Jack Dick took a phone call in his office, to be told that the British Museum had confiscated two paintings that were bought in his name that afternoon in Sotheby's Gallery, under the National Treasures Act. Jack took the news badly, telling the caller that the Limeys were nothing but a bunch of cheating hypocrites.

Once he put down the receiver, he took a stroll out into the front garden, admiring the ornate stone fountain that had once stood in the grounds of Belton House, Lincolnshire, England, and smiled to himself. They had taken the bait!

## Sotheby's Auction House, London - January 1967

'Do I hear fifty thousand? Come on gentlemen, who will give me fifty now. Paintings by Stubbs don't come this way very often. Come on, you know this is a golden opportunity........thank you sir.' An inner gasp of relief creased the auctioneer's face. 'Fifty thousand I am bid....' He pointed his gavel at a man in a sheepskin coat seated in the centre of the front row.

Unlike the previous few auctions, Jack had made the trip across the pond this time. It wasn't so much that he didn't trust a dealer to bid on his behalf but more that he had upset a few of them over the last few months. Brian had let him know well in advance that a Stubbs was coming up for sale and immediately Jack was aware that the 'powers that be' in England might not want it to stray too far from their rainy shores.

Over the last year, the name of Jack R Dick had become as well noted in the British art world as it had been in the Scottish cattle world five years earlier. 'A man who throw's his money around,' the papers had said. How little did they know. Jack may be prepared to spend more than others when he wanted something but, in every case, he was more than confident that whatever the cost, it would be repaid somehow.

Since his interest in the subject of sporting art some years back, a few dealers and investors had taken a look at some of their older masters and realised that perhaps they did have a place in history after all. This in general had driven up the prices and Jack had already made some handsome profit from his earlier purchases, should he wish to sell them - which he didn't.

Fearnley, Herring, Seymour and Aiken had been

particularly excellent painters, each through their own experience in working and living amongst horses. Jack had at least one copy by these artists in his collection. But George Stubbs had been in a league of his own. The master of masters.

Born in 1724, with the exception of Seymour, he was perhaps the founder of sporting art that others followed. A son of a leather merchant in Liverpool, Stubbs worked in the trade until his father's death when he was then apprenticed to a painter and engraver. By all accounts, the job wasn't for him, where he complained of having to copy the work of others, something he objected to. Jack could empathise with him on that. Working as a portrait painter, he studied human anatomy for a five year period, before making a trip to Italy to, in his own words, 'convince himself that nature was superior to art!' What happened next is as macabre as it is brilliant. In 1756, George Stubbs rented a farmhouse in East England and spent the next 18 months dissecting dead horses in order to study their anatomy. Rumours were that he, with the aid of his wife, even dragged huge parts of the horses upstairs where he had his own operating theatre. The stench must have been unbearable but the result was the publication of a book called 'The anatomy of the horse', a series of drawings which were subsequently seen by aristocrats of the time. It was soon established that his understanding of muscles and movement of the species superseded that of his forefathers. Three large paintings were commissioned as result, by the Duke of Richmond, one of his horse, 'Whistlejacket', and Stubbs soon became an artist of some merit.

The bay stallion, 'Goldfinger', had won the Spring race at Newmarket in 1769, almost exactly 200 years ago before it was painted by Stubbs in 1774 grazing with a mare and foal by a lake.

'Fifty five thousand,' called out the auctioneer. Without

hesitation, Jack waved his catalogue to bid sixty.

Next to him a rotund man in a brown tweed suit barely concealing the bulging buttons of a faded red waistcoat elbowed him in the ribs and muttered, 'They won't let you keep it!'

Jack said nothing, bidding again at seventy. By now, the room had fallen silent, with only the sound of the auctioneer's voice to be heard repeating the word a few times. One more bid from Jack sealed the deal at £72,000, which equated to 185,000 dollars. Once the hammer was banged down he stood up. 'We'll see about that, shall we?' he whispered into the fat man's ear.

For over a month, Jack had been waiting for this moment, as he brushed past a man in a grey suit standing in the doorway. 'Mister Henderson,' he nodded, smugly. The man scowled back at him.

Through his network of contacts, Jack had learned the exact state of the British Museum's accounts, right down to what they had in the bank. And thanks to them purchasing six pieces of art over the last few weeks, all of which had been supposedly destined for Jack's New York collection, what they had left in the bank was nowhere near enough to buy a Stubbs.

Jack tipped his hat at a few other men standing with Henderson. 'Good day, gentlemen.'

## Black Watch Farms - July 1968

'Click!'

It was no coincidence that the stable courtyard had not been locked on this clear summer night. Usually Bill Bohl was vigilant in his last check around the yard and paddocks before bed, regular as clockwork at eleven. Tonight was his night off, when they had two tickets to a theatre show in town, given to them by an anonymous benefactor who had praised his horsemanship and the way their animals had been looked after. Bill had accepted the ticket without questioning the source.

Now after midnight, a shadowy figure pulled open the heavy wooden door, shining his torch along the row of stables and looking into each one. One or two of the horses woke and a few made noises, but nothing out of the ordinary. This man was an expert and someone who knew how to instantly put a horse at ease. Selecting one particular door, he slid back the bolt and stepped inside, fastening the metal clip of a rope onto the horses halter. Once secure, he let out a low whistle.

Another man joined him, wearing a black woollen hat and dark clothing. He nodded to the first, taking the rope from him and leading the animal out into the night. Within five minutes, four more had gone the same way when the boy asked in a whisper. 'How many more, Sir?'

'Pack em as tight as you can, son. There'll be a full load.'

An hour later, the horse lorry pulled quietly out of the yard, refraining from turning on its headlights until it was fully on to the road. Behind the wheel, Bill Munson lit a cigarette and flipped the dead match out of the window.

'Let that be a lesson,' he said to the boy, and the world in general. 'No-one cheats me and gets away with it!'

## Pottstown, Pennsylvania - Fall 1967

Arthur Berman had single handedly started the Bermec Leasing company, initially called Berman Leasing, in the 1930s with a couple of trucks and an idea. Using bank's money it purchased semi trailers from manufacturers and then leased them out to trucking companies who were unable to secure loans themselves, at much higher interest rates. After a three to four year term, the trailers would have been fully paid for and owned by Berman, when he would then sell them off second-hand, making a tidy profit. From trailers, he progressed to trucks and by 1951 the company was incorporated on the New York Stock Exchange. Expanding at a vast rate, Berman's stock grew on the market, as they expanded the business to 65 maintenance terminal all across the US, funded by 15,000 shareholders. With a continually healthy balance sheet, the price of their shares rose steadily, reaching nearly a dollar share by 1966.

Believing he had grown the business as far as he could, Arthur and Herman L Meckler, chairman of the company, started to look around for other markets to expand into. An article about tax shelters had caught his eye in the Financial Times. Although this new guy, Nixon, from California had promised tax reduction if and when he ousted LBJ in the next presidential elections, tax was still a huge concern for Arthur. Sure, the current tax system had played into his hands over the last twenty years, when companies could use their lease payments to reduce tax rather than hanging on to a load of rolling stock. But the idea of the individual paying into a scheme and then picking up 'clean' money at the end of it had its appeal. The old man turned in his leather chair, as the intercom buzzed announcing an arrival.

'Ah, the great Jack Dick. I won't get up if you don't mind. Legs aren't what they used to be.'

Jack held out his hand to shake. 'Good of you to find me the time, Mister Berman.'

'Arthur. Please, call me Arthur.' He looked down at the glossy Black Watch Farms document on the desk in front of him. 'So, Jack, you came this way all on your own. I thought you would have lackys to do your leg work, eh? A busy man like you?' He looked up from the document and cut to the chase. 'So how much do I need to invest in this little scheme of yours to save myself from the taxman and make it worth my while, Jack?' The man's voice was a bit condescending, as though dealing with just another insurance salesman. Arthur had had many dealings with bankers, buyers, sellers, insurance men, and particularly with their lawyers. He felt it quite refreshing that the head of the company had arrived at his door, without any lawyers in sight, just to sell him an investment.

The next statement that Jack made changed the face of the conversation considerably. 'Thirty five million!'

After that, he thought the old man would have a coronary, as he spluttered into the coffee cup he was drinking from, spraying liquid on to the desk.

As the great salesman he was, Jack stayed silent, letting the words sink in and the man regroup himself. A whole minute went by with just the sound of the clock ticking, until eventually the old man spoke again. 'You want me to buy your business?'

Jack just grinned. 'You got it!'

'For thirty five million?'

'Yup.' He said, 'It's probably worth forty, but I'm not a greedy man!'

'In cash?' Arthur asked. He patted his pockets. 'Only I don't think I got that much on me right now!'

The two men both burst out laughing at the same time until Jack added. 'No, just in shares will be fine!' Settling back down again, he outlined the deal and the old man listened to his slick sales pitch, explaining how Black Watch Farms had expanded right across the US, with multiple revenue streams and room for more. Growing to like this young man, Arthur eventually held up a hand, stopping him mid flow and standing to his feet. He made his way unsteadily to a drinks cabinet and pulled out a decanter and two glasses.

'You got some balls, Jack Dick,' he said, offering him a glass. 'What say I get Meckler to have a look at your proposition, see what you're sitting on? Not promising anything, but we can sure take a look.'

Jack agreed to give Bermec's lawyers open access to his books and invited him to come and take a tour of the place. 'Why not come up for the weekend, I'll send my private plane. Bring Mrs Berman as well. You got a runway here out in these sticks?'

# PART III

## Dunnellen Hall, Greenwich, New York - July 1968

'Darling, what a fabulous party,' a lady dressed in a long velvet gown pulled tightly around her middle, lifted another glass of champagne from a passing tray. Her husband, clad in a red and white striped vest, under what appeared to be a chainmail overall wiped the sweat from his brow, nodding. His wife looked him up and down. 'Brian! You haven't lost your sword have you,' her eyes narrowed. 'That has to go back tomorrow. You really should be more careful.' The husband mentioned that it had been taken to the cloakroom by one of the waiters as he thought it was a bit cumbersome to carry around all evening. His wife wasn't listening. 'Have you seen him yet?'

'Seen who?' he replied, quietly.

'This Dick man!' She was looking around, smiling to a couple she knew and giving a little wave. 'Look, there's the wotsanames, and they'r coming this way,' she hissed under her breath.

'Betty and John from the white house on the corner of Round Hill Road,' he reminded her. Sometimes he thought the woman would forget his name, let alone that of her neighbours.

She was already greeting the couple with hugs and air kisses. 'Betty, Darling. You look fabulous.' Brian thought she looked uncomfortable, but he didn't say so, as he shook hands with his neighbour. The two exchanged a look that suggested they would rather be in their own garden, wearing something cooler. 'I was just saying, what a fabulous party.'

Betty wasn't so much impressed by the party, but the

house itself. 'Have you seen what he's done with the place? All that marble. It's voluptuous.'

'Must have more money than sense,' Brian offered, in a mutter.

'Oh you accountants are all the same, looking at the cost of things,' his wife scolded him again. Then she whispered to her new found companion, 'which one is he?' Before Betty could answer, she added, 'Oh my god, isn't that Mike Nichols, the movie director, over there! The Graduate was so good, I thought I was going to die!'

Brian wandered off towards the bar, leaving the women gossiping. And they weren't the only ones. After collecting a glass of beer from another passing waiter, he made his way to a stone seat in the garden and sat down. It was a splendid party, he had to agree. The whole 'Camelot' theme seemed to work well, some people just had a knack of organising these things. A massive high topped tent adorned the centre of the garden, striped in red and green, where a band was playing. The waiters all wore the same uniform, again in red and green, including woollen tights. Brian reckoned they would be feeling this hot July evening heat as much as he was.

His eyes strayed to the house itself, which looked magnificent in the glow of orange spotlights, with its mock Tudor turrets fitting the evening's theme. He knew this house and had been here before to a party by the previous owner. When he had got home he had done some research on the place, just to pass the time now he was retired.

It had been built in 1918 by a man called Daniel Reid at a cost of one million dollars, an absolute fortune back then. Set on top of Round Hill in twenty five acres, with its sweeping views over to Long Island Sound, he constructed it for to his daughter, Rhea, as a wedding present when she married Dan Topping, who went on to be the owner of the New York Yankees. They had lived there until the fifties and the house was nicknamed

Topping Estate, with that part of Round Hill Road taking on the same name. After that, nobody seemed to stay there very long. Some steel magnate bought it but later his business empire collapsed leaving him ruined and the house lay empty for a few years. Then the last owner had been much more interesting, being the former showgirl, pinup and, some say, call girl, Gregg Sherwood. Having had her half-naked body splashed over the front page of many magazines she had married the heir to the Dodge motoring fortune, Horace Dodge Jnr, and boy, did she know how to spend his cash. Lavish parties here had been hosted for the rich and famous, not unlike this one. From what he understood, a couple of years back he filed for divorce but then died before it was settled and she got the lot. After this latest guy bought it, he heard that Sherwood, or Dodge, had married a policeman half her age.

Thinking about it, there had been a history of misfortune linked to this place.

He hadn't met the owner yet, but guessed he was another hotshot, the way he had thrown money around, buying statues and chandeliers by the dozen. He had heard the man had even built a 5000 bottle wine cellar; who the hell drank 5000 bottles of wine? Ran some kind of tax scam in New York, so the local rumour went, something to do with cows. Brian went to take a closer look at the place, where a bunch of guys were gathering near the entrance, all dressed in these outrageous costumes.

'Brian Watson, Sothebys,' one man was saying, introducing himself.

'Bernie Madoff, market trader,' replied another.

The host certainly seemed to have a lot of connections. Brian imagined his wife's eagle eye seeking out faces from the entertainment world that she would have seen in Vanity Fair. One of her friends had been convinced that

Frankie Sinatra was on the guest list. One of the two men offered him a cigar as he reached them but he declined. 'Say, haven't they got any air-conditioning in this place?' The two men smiled.

## 21 Club, Manhattan, New York - February 1969

21, West 52nd Street, Manhattan, had a pretty interesting history itself. Built during the twenties, it was widely documented how the 21 Club was run as a speakeasy by two cousins and was known as 'Jack and Charlies.' If history was to be believed, the reason they never got caught during prohibition was, as well as tip-offs from the police, a series of levers were constructed into the bar that, if a raid took place, would swivel the shelves over, dumping all the bottles into the sewer below. There had also been a secret wine cellar accessed through a door hidden in a brick wall which could only be opened if a skewer was inserted into one of the bricks at the correct angle. A story goes that Mayor Jimmy Walker and his mistress were locked in the cellar during a raid one time but he managed to get to a telephone and called the chief of police, instructing him to get all the federal vehicles towed off the street. The feds not only found no booze during the raid but when they went outside their cars were gone too!

Since those days, the 21 Club had become one of the most exclusive in New York, where presidents and the rich and famous went to dine and socialise. Hitchcock, Bogart, Hemingway and others even had tables named after them in the swanky restaurant which served some of the best food in town. Just the previous week, Frankie Sinatra and Jackie Onassis had been photographed leaving the place. The old wine cellar, which actually ran underneath number 19 next door, had been turned into a private room where parties or business meetings could be held out of the earshot of other diners.

Jack and Lynda liked the 21 Club for its connection to the sporting world. Horse trainers and owners would frequent the place as well as well as baseball players and other familiar faces from the world of sport. He and his wife frequently dined at the club but tonight was strictly business.

'I'm telling you Jack, these folks are playing for real!' Despite no longer have financial ties with Black Watch, he had kept Joe Moretti on his payroll, just to keep the final loose ends of the deal tidied away.

The deal selling Black Watch Farms to the Bermec Leasing Corporation had gone through pretty smoothly, when the company paid out 26 million in share bonds in exchange for the whole shebang, which was now managing 30,000 head of cattle across 20 states. Of this payout, as a main shareholder, Jack received five million. Although he knew the solid history of the Bermec company, call it a premonition, but Jack felt they may have a few troubled times ahead, so he cashed his in, pretty much immediately. He had since bought Dunnellen Hall and its estate for one and a half million and spent a whole heap of money turning it into the opulent palace it had become. Using his contacts, containers of artefacts had been bought and shipped from England including antique furniture, chandeliers, statues and other genuine pieces of Tudor history. By re-laying all the marble floors and restoring the ornate cornicing of the high walls, Jack had started to fill the great house with his real passion, sporting art. To top it all, he got a Rolls Royce.

The tone of his accountant, generally an upbeat sort of guy, sounded grim.

'Come on, Joe. They got nothing on us.' Jack replied in his usual confident tone.

'You can't keep denying it all, Jack. Not to me anyway. I am on your side, pal. The feds are all over us now. Meckler over at Bermec is screeching at us. Says the whole thing was rigged from the start. According to him, the cattle were worth less than a quarter of what we sold them. And he says we missed out in telling him about the loans, let alone the million dollars we owe to the farmers.'

'We owe?' Jack actually smiled. 'We don't owe nothing, Joe. They did their looking, and then they bought what they saw. If they didn't look hard enough, well, that's a real shame for them.'

Joe raised his eyes to the vaulted ceiling, breathing heavily. 'How do you sleep at night, Jack?'

At that Jack put down his knife and fork and stared directly at his colleague. 'Like a baby, Joe. I sleep like a newborn at night coz I ain't done nothing wrong.' He picked up the fork again, putting a piece of steak in his mouth. 'So, I didn't tell them a few minor details. There're big boys, they'll cope. Meckler never liked me from the getgo, so he's bound to say a few nasty things. What else is new.'

'You wanna know what I think. I think they will come after us, Jack. I already got requests for the Feds to take a look in my office.' He held up his hand as Jack opened his mouth. 'Don't worry, Jack, we got a good paper shredder. Way I see it, Bermec wont hold that company together more than a year and if it goes down, they are gonna come hunting.'

Jack was still dismissive. 'Black Watch was a perfectly profitable company when we sold it. If they don't know how to run it, they shouldn't have bought it. And that's the bottom line!'

Joe sat quietly for a minute, eating his dinner and sipping a glass of high grade red wine. 'What about you, Jack?' he said eventually. 'I heard rumours. Is it true?'

'Got nothing to do with you, Joe. Don't get involved.'

Joe looked at him. 'Jack, I'm your friend. You wanna

tell me what's going on?'

Jack let his guard slip, just for a moment, running his hands though his hair. 'Is it true, that they are suing me for embezzlement?' He sighed. 'Sure it's true, Joe. They say I stole money. Can you believe that? Me, steal money? Look at me, I am one of the richest guys in the state. You think I would steal, Joe?'

Joe shook his head, letting the air clear before asking quietly. 'How much?'

'Three million, goddamnit. They are saying I stole three million dollars!'

## Dunnellen Hall, Greenwich - November 1969

It had been Lynda's idea to install electric gates at Topping. Unlike the dusty track that led to the ranch, where folks would turn up day and night, often knocking on the door of the main house at all hours instead of visiting the farm manager. Dunnellen Hall did have gates on its tarmac driveway when they bought the place, a huge pair of wrought iron ones that weighed a couple of tons, but these had rusted up and, even when working freely, took all of one's effort to open and close. Now a push button in the house was all it took for them to slowly swing open on hydraulic motors. As the entrance was some way from the big house, a camera had been installed looking over them, showing any arrivals on a small screen in Jack's office, as well as one in a janitor's hut in the grounds.

It was on this that he recognised the first sign of trouble, seeing a tall man pressing the buzzer.

'I'm here to see Jack R Dick,' the man said into speaker, wringing his hands to keep out the cold.

'What's your business with him?' the janitor asked.

Jack watched the visitor on the TV screen, taking a deep breath. 'Tell him it's his father!' said Sam Dick, agitatedly. In a few seconds his phone rang, the guy stating that his father was at the gate and should be let him in. 'No!' said Jack, calmly, and put down the receiver. Again he watched the man's reaction when the news reached him; him returning to the open door of the car and speaking to its passengers.

Next it was his mother's turn, pressing the buzzer again, her high heels unsteady on the icy driveway. 'Can you tell him that his mother is here too, and she is cold! And also his brother Elliot and his new wife.'

Jack knew his brother had gotten married and, when he received the invite, had sent him a heap of money to pay for the wedding in way of reply. He hadn't met the new wife but, based on what he knew of Elliot, she wouldn't be anything special, just some floozy from the Everglades, so he had heard. Again the phone rang. 'Yes!' he snapped. 'Tell them I am busy.'

This time, watching the monitor again, he let out a sigh, as the old man started shouting, clouds of steam rising off him in the cold morning air. Jack turned away and shut off the sound, returning to reading a document on his desk.

He had enough troubles just now, with the Securities Commission serving him with an indictment that contained some quite accurate accusations. Somehow they had gotten wind of his overseas bank account and were demanding access. They had also managed to bend Joe Moretti's arm and get a look at a few files he held. For the first time since the issue was mentioned, Jack had started to get a little worried. Word of the indictment had gotten out to Bermec, and Meckler was now threatening him too, adding to the concerns they already had about the real value of the business when he purchased it. Bermec were big players and had some pretty heavyweight lawyers in their armoury. Not only that, but they got the backing of quite a few of his previous clients, making his phone so hot that his secretary had threatened to quit on the grounds of all the abuse she was getting. A pay raise soon fixed that problem but some of the calls got through and Jack was having to handle the situation carefully. Some of these guys kept bad company.

Of course, the old man wouldn't know any of this; in fact his wife Lynda only had a few sketchy details. As far as she was concerned, Jack was absolutely innocent and she would make sure she said so to anyone wagging their tongue on the subject. And he was innocent, Jack advocated that himself. Sure he had lifted a few payments directly into his account in Switzerland, but that was only to avoid the tax man. The business was his own; he had started it and he was directly responsible for its success. As far as he was concerned, the profits that Black Watch generated were his to keep - and if a company that could help hundreds of folks save paying income tax, then it sure should be able to work the same deal on its owner.

What was it Joe had said at their last meeting? 'I can't see them holding the business together for more than a year.' With news reports of a financial recession on its way, that might well be true. Couple that with Congress reforming its income tax laws, and Bermec may not just have the queue of Black Watch investors to their door that Jack had experienced. Now clients had to hold on to cattle for two years instead of just one before writing off capital gains tax too, that certainly wouldn't help.

Still that was no longer Jack's concern and that is pretty much what he told them. Times change, things move on. I moved on. So should you.

And so should that man at his front gate who, Jack witnessed on the TV screen, was now picking up rocks and throwing them over the gate in temper. His next call was a fairly simple one. '911. Yes officer, someone is trying to deface my property. Could you have them arrested, please!'

## Greenwich Village, New York - 1971

It felt good to be back in The Village again. Since his early days the place had changed a lot, becoming fashionable to young artists who gathered there in trendy bars, exchanging ideas and ideals while blowing their minds with drugs. This was the centre of New York's revolution, a kind of fallout from California's summer of love a few years before. Although far removed from some of the seedier clubs downtown, it had also been a bit more contentious of late as the centre of the city's gay community, something that was not widely accepted in the States. Jack thought back to the Anvil Club and whatever went on in the basement there, some of which he had witnessed with his own eyes. Recent riots in Greenwich Village had seen gay activists clash with police grabbing some news headlines for their movement. Although still only in his thirties, Jack somehow felt old amongst this modern eclectic mix of artists and revolutionaries as he checked the street for the address he was looking for.

It was a young guy he had met at the 21 Club that had given him this contact. The guy was a wheeler dealer who had ears and eyes in all sorts of places and liked to hang out with Jack if he could, always eager to please for a few back-handed notes. Jack had taken one of the Sedans for this little trip; it wasn't the sort of place where you would park a Rolls on the curb.

The apartment block looked like it had once been a warehouse, clad in old brick with rows of big square windows. He rang the buzzer and a voice answered telling him to come on up, top floor. Jack looked around, checking he hadn't been followed, before opening the door and taking the steel stairway. A thin young man with wiry red hair met him on the top landing. He looked like he had just woken up. In fact, by the look of his eyes, he may even still be half asleep, wrapped in a blue towelling dressing-gown that had seen better days.

Jack reached out his hand to shake. 'Jack.'

'Call me Peter.' The voice was gruff, with tones of European. Maybe French.

Jack followed him through into an apartment which was vast, covering most of the top floor of the building. At the far end, an unmade bed lay strewn with white cotton sheets, the floor around it scattered with clothes.

Three huge windows drew in the sunlight in rays across bare wooden floorboards, glinting a reflection off a pile of paint tins. The main focus of the room was at least half a dozen wooden easels, standing in a random fashion like a disorganised graveyard. Each one contained half-finished paintings, some near complete, some just pencil lines. Peter dropped on to a couch and watched his visitor, in his open neck shirt and polished shoes. He sniffed periodically, as though his nose was bothering him. It was a common habit of artists; too much time spent around paint fumes although Jack guessed that it was more that fumes that went up this guy's nostrils.

'Tony said it would be worth my while,' he said.

Jack studied the canvasses, checking some of the lines. 'He said you were good.'

Peter just nodded, not feeling the need to quantify the statement. 'I do OK.'

Under the window a few more canvasses leant against the wall, the front one of which he recognised. It was Renoir's Cauliflowers, not the easiest work to copy. Jack checked it over and then flipped a few more forward. A Corot caught his eye. Everyone did Corot. Eventually he turned to the artist. 'Do you know who Stubbs is, Peter?' He watched the man's eyes.

Peter's expression turned to a grin. 'Sporting art? I had you more down as a Renaissance man, or maybe Rembrandt.'

'Rembrandt?' It was Jack's turn to smile. 'No, no, far too dull!'

'You got it with you?'

Jack made a tutting sound. 'It? What makes you think there is only one?'

At the far end of the room the bed moved. 'Don't mind her, she doesn't speak English,' Peter explained, as a naked girl revealed herself from between the sheets and stood up, her eyes half closed. She padded off towards a bathroom and Jack watched her perfect body disappear.

Peter's interest turned back to Jack's last question. 'How many are we talking about?'

'Twenty, twenty five, maybe? You can start with an easy one, by Richard Ansdell, and show me what you can do. I will get it checked over and then we will sell it. If it passes muster, you get the job.'

Peter stood up, pulling the cord tight on his robe. 'It's not the pictures that are difficult, but the bloody signatures.'

'Well. You had better get practicing. It's in my trunk.' Jack started heading for the door, beckoning the man to follow.

Peter stood his ground for a short while. 'I'm expensive.'

'I rather expected you would be, Peter,' Jack said over his shoulder. 'There's a bundle of cash in there too.'

## The Anvil Club, 14th Street, New York - 1971

There was never a sign over the door saying who owned The Anvil Club but it was common knowledge that the place was pretty much outside the law. As the permissive sixties gave way to the unregulated seventies, so sex and porn moved from the seedy back streets into mainstream. The Anvil had a heterosexual reputation, making it slightly different from many of the other all gay clubs around the city and Joe Garrecci liked to keep it that way. His father Tony had been one of the original heavyweights in the town but had always been a man of principle, prepared to listen to both side of the story. During the mid sixties, when tempers among the mob got a little heated, the old man's voice had been one of reason, suggesting if the New York Mafia couldn't all get along, then maybe it was time to divide the city up between them. That they did but at the expense of quite a few heads, his old man's included.

Back then The Anvil had just been a lock up, tucked away down a side avenue and it was Tony's idea to open it up as a private club in 1969, to begin with vetting its members and their guests. That decision had proved to be a stroke of genius, when the police department came calling. They were on the payroll, of course, pretty much every one of the NYPD took a weekly envelope, but it was the roster of names that proved to be a valuable asset to Joe's standing amongst the firm. That and the tiny TV cameras that had been installed around the place. Over the next couple of years, prostitution became a very handsome business, mainly overlooked by the authorities, many of whom used their personal services. Joe extended his empire into a couple more establishments as well as dozens of girls and boys on the streets, each of whom paid him a cut of their trade. And then there were the movies shot in the basement and shown in a 30-seat theatre at three bucks a go, mainly to men in long overcoats. Couple that with sales of liquor, plus magazines and accessories in the shop, and Garrecci was fast becoming a rich man.

He glanced at a few screens in front of him, each one with the sound turned down. Twosomes, threesomes, bondage, transvestites and lesbians, in fact pretty much any sordid act you could possibly imagine showed across those monitors on a daily basis. At first he had used to hit the 'record' button and saved the tapes to play at parties with a few buddies but the novelty of watching continuous sexual acts soon wore off. Nowadays the only time he recorded anything was when it was done by someone of note, such as the police chief, mayor or occasional Senator quenching their sexual urges on boys half their age.

'Send him up!' As a second generation American, Joe had all but lost his Sicilian accent, as he spoke into the intercom and then watched a well dressed man in his thirties follow one of his staff up a narrow corridor. The man looked nervous and not the sort who usually frequented this place. 'Mister Dick, come on in.' He stood to shake Jack's hand. 'Can I offer you anything?' Joe indicated to a decanter sitting on the table, next to a couple of silver boxes containing cigarettes and other substances. He watched Jack's brief glance at the monitors on the desk, gauging his reaction to seeing two men each with a head between the legs of the other. It wasn't the look of a man who was at ease with such liberal goings on.

Jack shook his head at the offer, taking a seat opposite the desk so that he could no longer see the screens. His discomfort showed as he adjusted his posture in his seat a couple of times.

'So, you brought my money, Mister Dick?' Joe made a point of looking the man up and down. 'Only, I don't see thirty grand in cash in your soft hands?'

Jack returned his stare, choosing his words. 'You'll get you money back, Mister Garrecci. Not just your money but a lot more besides. I am sure you are a man who likes to make a profit.' Working most of his life as a salesman, Jack was used to handing out lines like that, knowing everyone always wanted more. And yet, in this case, the payoff needed to be bigger - and lucky.

'My money and more?' Joe's eyes narrowed. 'I already got my money and more coming back, Mister Dick. I lend you twenty, you give me back thirty. I think that is what we called a deal?' He let out a sigh, his stale breath battling against the smell of flowery aftershave. 'Are you saying you don't know how to keep a deal?'

'To the contrary, I have a better deal to offer you.' Jack met his stare again. 'How about I give you forty?'

'I'm listening.'

'Forty thousand, but not in cash.'

## Dunnellen Hall - 1973

Slamming the phone down, Jack had had enough. Couldn't anyone bring him some good news? He reached over and poured himself a brandy, carrying it out from his office into the wooden panelled library.

At least this room was still full of art, if not all his favourites. His eyes rested on a Camille Corot and he smiled. Corot never got out much and nearly all his paintings were of people and places in and around Paris. This one, 'Ville d'Avray' was of a woman standing near the Seine. Jack considered himself a busy man, even now when he was supposedly retired, but he wondered how Corot had managed to paint so many pictures in one lifetime. His work was simple, which was its appeal to many, but simplicity made it an easy target to copy. Jack reckoned with enough time on his hands and the right paint, he could just about copy this one himself, although in his version there would be a few black cows grazing down by the shore! There was a story in the art world about Corot that said, of the 2000 works he painted, 6000 hung in Texas alone! They had the original of this one hanging in the National Gallery in NYC - or so they thought. Jack knew different!

He moved to the next frame, breathing in its splendid colours. James Seymour was much more his scene. 'Sir Roger Burgoyne Riding Badger' was the inscription painted in the bottom left corner. As he looked at it, he could feel the horse moving in unison with the hound by its side, almost hearing its footsteps on the gravel drive below. Jack thought Sir Roger displayed such an air of eloquence as he looked out from the picture and yet somehow he seemed troubled. Maybe they were trying to take away his estate too.

Jack considered the latest phone call. In the last years of Black Watch he had managed to secure a loan for 800 grand from a finance company to keep them afloat. In short, he hadn't been wholly truthful with the details of the security he put up for it and now they were coming after him, guns blazing. Normally he would have traded his way out of it, the same as he'd always done. Find a company somewhere, take share options by putting up some guarantees, seduce a young trader to start pushing the stocks, put word around the market that these were hot, then cash them in before the top. Making money was easy if you knew how, and you didn't even need cash to do it.

But he couldn't do that now, not since his asshole father had stuck his oar in. Twenty million, that's what the old bastard had sued him for. If it had just been a few mill he could have worked his way out of it. But twenty? Well that got the attention of the DA, didn't it. That's how it worked in the world: maybe it was the old man that had taught him that. Chuck a few pennies in the fountain and nobody takes much notice, but throw in a suitcase full of used notes, and the whole town comes running. Now the story that Jack had shafted his whole family just rode on the back of whatever other bullshit accusations were being thrown his way. Eventually they had put on a restraining order that stopped him trading, stopped him spending anything in fact.

And then there was the IRS getting in on the act, looking for one and a half million. Well if he was under restraint, he couldn't pay them, could he.

Just a week had gone by since he heard that Black Watch had gone down the tube. When Jack struggled to make the figures stack up, he was pretty sure Meckler and his boys wouldn't manage to keep bailing out the boat.

And now it looked as though they were in trouble too. Bermec share price dropped from nearly one dollar down below 20 cents, that would get a few creditors jumpy. Maybe the whole outfit would fold. It didn't bother Jack too much, he had sold his shares long ago.

There had also been the small matter of borrowing money from some more unscrutible people, such as Joe Garrecci. For now he had that one taken care of and the guy seemed happy enough with the deal, accepting a painting by Aiken which would more than cover his debt. But when you borrowed anything from anyone of wealth in this city, there was always the danger that the mob were in the backroom somewhere. It was also common knowledge that some of these guys didn't fuck around when it came to getting repaid, or getting even.

He put the phone call from his mind, turning his eyes back to the art.

Eventually he reached the centrepiece of the room and thought back to how he had managed to buy it, outwitting the stubborn old boys at the British Museum. What a load of stuffed old pricks they were. Did they really think they could keep all their treasures in a box under the stairs? He let out a laugh, tracing his eyes over the magnificent outline of 'Goldfinger'.

Lynda silently watched him from the doorway but Jack felt her eyes on him and turned.

'You know it's for the best, Jack,' she said quietly.

'Yeah, I know.' He glanced at her, trying not to focus on the empty space on the wall behind her shoulder where one of his masterpieces had hung until yesterday. 'It's today, right?'

She nodded and then turned away. Lynda had stood right by his side for the last 14 years. Just there in the shadows, bringing up the kids and keeping them safe and warm. A close family, and yet so distant that somehow he felt he hardly knew them at all. Business had been his real wife, and money his mistress. Today they would arrive to take away the last of its fruits, leaving her exposed and naked.

Today was the day they came for 'Goldfinger'. Soon would be the moment of truth.

## Greenwich Village, New York - September 1973

Peter pressed the buzzer to release the door downstairs. He didn't know this visitor but the voice said it was business, and Peter was always happy to talk business.

When he answered the door to his apartment, that confident thought evaporated, to be replaced by something slightly more fearful.

Of the two men who entered, it was difficult to establish which one was the more frightening. One wore a trilby hat, spoke in a menacing Italian-Bronx accent: even had a dark scar across his cheek to reinforce the look.

The other sported something equally terrifying. A handgun!

Eyes darting left and right, Peter considered which way he should run but was way too late as the heftier of the two grabbed him around the neck.

'Right, Peter, we would like a little word with you?' the man grunted into his left ear.

'Peter is not my real name...' Peter already felt a trickle of warmth running down the inside of his leg. 'Who are you, what do you want?'

'I don't give a fuck what your real name is, son.' The man pushed him backwards, onto a chair his pal had positioned there. 'We ask the questions, you give the answers, capiche?'

The other man waved the barrel of the gun in the air in front of him, as though conducting a tune to himself. A smile came over his face as he pointed it down to Peter's crunch, then back to his head, as if to ask which part of him would prefer to take the bullet.

'You've been a naughty boy, Peter.' Joe Garrecci was looking at the paintings sitting on easels in various states of completion. 'You've upset a few people with your little racket, you have.' He pulled out a knife from his pocket, flicking open the blade. 'Because of you, some people are getting confused. Some of my friends, Peter.' The speed he swiped the blade across a canvass depicting a man on horseback was as immeasurable as it was terrifying, as the two half of it peeled open like a tin of sardines. Even his pal winced at the sight.

'What do you want?' Peter managed. This got him a slap from the barrel of a gun across his face, drawing a tiny droplet of blood from just below his eye.

'What we want, Peter whatever-the-fuck-your-name-is,' Joe pushed his face down to Peter's level. 'Is to know what is real. We want to know which of these paintings is worth a lotta money and which ones are worth fuck all?' Garrecci stood upright again, taking a deep breath.

'You're not going to kill me?' The wet stain around Peter's crutch was expanding as he pleaded.

'Kill you?' Both men laughed. 'Now why would we do that?' Joe looked to his companion. 'We don't do that, no more, do we?'

'Nah, Boss.' When the man spoke for this first time, his accent was more Hispanic, Mexican maybe. 'S'more fun cutting them up!'

'You know, you are one lucky son of a bitch, Peter,' Joe continued, the knife blade now back under Peter's chin. 'Rico here likes to cut offa da fingers. It's his speciality. But you need those fingers just now. Because, once you have told us good from bad, you are gonna have to get to work.' He put the blade away in his pocket. 'So let's start with a mutual friend of ours, Mister Dick.'

Peter was about to deny that he had ever heard of him but then thought better of it. 'What do you want to know?'

## Sotheby's Auction house, London - January 1974

'Do I hear two hundred thousand? Come on gentlemen, who will give me two hundred thousand pounds. Paintings by Stubbs don't come this way very often. Especially not 'Goldfinger'. Come on now, you know this is a golden opportunity........thank you, Sir.' An inner gasp of relief creased the auctioneer's face. 'Two hundred I am bid....'

Out front, the auction room seats were all taken, as was the standing room, and at least another 200 people were listening from the hallway. The buzz in the air was almost electric, as everyone scrambled to get a piece of the action. During the company's long existence, this was one of the most important sales of sporting art it had ever held. Not for the first time in his life Jack R Dick was writing history. In the front row, collectors from around the globe sat patiently, sharing the spoils like vultures on a wire. Among them, Paul Mellon and Mike Nichols were watched very carefully by the 'establishment'. This time the Brits were ready.

Jack and Lynda heard the sale over an intercom in a small office at the back of the building. 'Let them take my art, it was all only borrowed, really,' he told to himself. As he listened he considered the passion he had for the wonderful pieces that had been in his possession for only a short time, trebling in value in the process. 'We buy it, we nurture it, and then we give it back to history,' he sighed out loud, 'keeping only the memories.'

What he didn't add was that, in his case, he had kept a little more than the memories of it.

London businessman Charles Clore was at the back of the room, dressed in an immaculate blue suit. He and Jack went back a long way, back to the days of Aberdeen Angus cattle when Clore had his own herd in England and had also once paid a record price for a bull in Perth. Funny thing, coincidence.

One bid was all it took. 'Two hundred thousand pounds!'

## 21 Club, Manhattan - January 1974

While sitting with Lynda in a low leather chair, Jack had been discussing the recent sale of his paintings, which had totalled over three million dollars. And that was only half of them. Watson had suggested that there were too many of one type to put in a single sale, and that they should spread the sale over two years. However, the capital it had raised would allow him to pay off his creditors, especially now they had the house on the market as well. Things were looking up. Sure he still had the indictment hanging over him and the trial date had been set. But they wouldn't get him into jail, he was pretty confident of that. Too many people would have to talk to do that, and he was pretty sure they wouldn't.

'You know I'll bounce back, don't you,' he said quietly. His wife smiled. She did. 'Money is made round to go round. This art world is an open chequebook,' he continued, waving his arm to order another brandy. 'I can buy and sell this stuff all day long.' In his mind he imagined a new world, where he would buy out gallery after gallery, trading paintings and blurring the lines between real and false. He was slurring his words slightly, the brandy kicking in.

'Maybe you've had enough, Jack?' His wife put a hand on his arm but he pulled it away.

'Enough?' he said. *'Enough of this bullshit, yes! But today I feel like a stock on the up tick. I have bottomed out and I'm on the way up. I'm heading for a peak. I've been known to have the Midas touch. I have walked in the rain without getting wet and there is no reason why I can't do it again. You know why I make money? Because I decide to make money.'* A few eyes turned towards him, and the waiter held off bringing the drink until a more opportune moment. *'And right now I have decided on a new goal. I made $1 million by the time I was 20, $20 million at 30, $50 million at 40. Well, now I am going to shoot for $100 million, no, make that $200 million, by the time I'm 50. People say with luck I might be able to make it. I know I will!'*

He sat quietly for a minute, feeling a little queasy. The waiter brought the drink and set it down on a side table. 'Hey Johnny,' he said, 'you got a couple of Bufferin?' Jack rubbed his hand across his forehead. 'I don't feel so good.'

Minutes later, the two of them climbed into the back of his black limousine parked out front. As they pulled out on to the New England Freeway, a motorbike pulled alongside the car, its rider looking in through the darkened window, steering the bike with one hand, his other one reaching inside his jacket.

Jack pulled his hand to his chest.

Ow,' he said, 'that really hurt!'

Twenty minutes later, Jack R Dick was pronounced dead on arrival at Bellevue Hospital on East 24th Street.

The death certificate stated the cause of death as heart failure.

THE END

## Prologue

**Lynda Dick** died 7 years after her husband of a cancer-related illness. She is survived by her children Lori and Johnny.

At 60,000 guineas (63,000 pounds) **Lindertis Evulse** still holds the record for the most expensive Angus bull sold by auction in Britain, some 60 years later. Essedium of Dounside (54,000gns) and Erisco of Ballachin (40,000gns) also hold second and third place, all three of which went to Black Watch Farms.

**George Wallace** remained governor of Alabama for two non consecutive terms up until 1968. He sought Democrat nomination in 3 presidential elections in 1964, 1972 and 1976 as well as running for President for the American Independence Party in 1968. Wallace survived an assassination attempt in 1972 that left him paralyzed and saw out the rest of his life in a wheelchair.

**Peter Revson** went on to win the British and Canadian Grand Prix in 1973 for Maclaren, before being killed during a practice session for the 1974 South African Grand Prix. He is to date the last American to win a Formula One Grand Prix. His brother was also killed on the race track a few years later.

**Dave Canning** went on to work with one single Angus bull from Canada called Camilla Chance 37T, known better as Canadian Colossal, breeding an entire Angus herd around its genetics. His annual 'Colossal sale' in Virginia was visited by breeders from all over the world, notching up some of the highest averages the breed had seen. Offspring of this bull were purchased by a breeder in Ireland, and later Scotland, in the late seventies, the first Angus to cross back over the Atlantic in history. The bull's influence can still be seen in some of the top cattle in Europe to this day.

'The Graduate', directed by **Mike Nichols,** is hailed by many as one of the greatest films of all time for which he was received an Academy Award. During his career Mike's work was rarely far from the limelight with films including Catch-22, Postcards from the Edge, and Closer, as well as directing stage shows such as Monty Python's Spamalot. Mike became a personal friend to some of the best known names in Hollywood. His love of horses never left him, both on the hoof and on canvas, and he was a highly successful breeder of Arabian horses, often advised by Bill Bohl. When he died in 2014, most of Hollywood turned out for his funeral.

Having lost $85,000 in Black Watch, **Bernie Madoff**'s first look at a Ponzi scheme inspired him to take the idea to another level, something which he built up over the next 20 years. In 2011, he was arrested for 11 felonies concluding he had defrauded investors of billions of dollars in undoubtedly the biggest financial scandal the world had ever seen.

**Dunnellen Hall** was eventually sold by Lynda Dick to oil and steel tycoon Ravi Tikkoo for 3 million dollars. However, Ravi's wife did not enjoy the house which she, and a good few other owners including Lynda Dick, felt was an unlucky place. He sold it to Harry and Leona Helmsley in 1983 for 11 million, who renovated it again, adding two more swimming pools! After Harry being indicted for tax evasion, Leona inherited Harry's property fortune when he died suddenly, which included a lease on the Empire State Building, estimated at 5.3 billion dollars. She later served 18 months sentence of a 16 year term in jail for fraudulent offences. When Leona died of heart failure in 2007, the property was put on the market for $70m but only realised $35m due to the market crash. The new owners kept it just two years before reselling the doomed house for $43m.

**Charles Clore,** later Sir Charles, was a London based financier who owned a considerable business empire including Jowett Cars Ltd, Lewis Retail group which included Selfridges stores, The British Shoe Corp, as well as vast swathes of east London properties. A well connected man, he was rumoured to mix with the notorious Kray Twins and was named as a client of hooker Christine Keeler in the Promfumo scandal. In 1980, thieves broke into his apartment in Monaco and made off with 19 paintings including works by Renoir, Monet and Picasso. Later it was found that the break-in had been staged and the butler was imprisoned for the crime. Money he donated to the Tate Gallery in London helped build a wing named after him which now houses the largest collection of works by JW Tuner. On Clore's death he was sued by the Inland Revenue for tax evasion.

The 1974 sale of Goldfinger by **George Stubbs** was the most expensive sporting art painting sold up until that date. The value of his work increased so dramatically over the next half century that, in 2011, a painting entitled 'Gimcrack on Newmarket Heath' (1765) was sold for a record £22.5 million ($32m) at Christie's in London to an anonymous buyer.

## Final word

Peter was not the real name of the forger which has been protected for legal reasons. During his career he has admitted to copying over 2000 paintings and claims that dozens of his works hang in galleries around the world, mistaken for originals by top professionals. He has no intention of revealing which ones they are.

After being arrested by the FBI in 2003, they were unable to convict him of any crimes.

## Facts

The majority of this book is based on true facts after a few years of extensive research by the authors.

The words in italics on the last page are Jack Dick's actual last words, witnessed and later transcribed to the coroner by the waiter at 21 Club.

Although the author has made every effort to ensure that the information in this book was correct at press time, the author (and publisher) do not assume and hereby disclaim any liability to any party for any loss, damage, or disruption caused by errors or omissions, whether such errors or omissions result from negligence, accident, or any other cause.

# The Author

**Andy Frazier**

Having had careers in livestock breeding, sales and computing in middle England, **Andy Frazier** moved to France nearly 10 years ago where he has now written in excess of 30 books on a variety of subjects. It was during research into a large volume about the history of cattle that Jack Dick first took his attention and, the more he uncovered, the more he realised that this story just had to be told.

# Acknowledgements

- Ray Kennedy, New York (SI)
- Hugh Hildersley, Sotheby's
- Bill Bohl
- Patti Douglas
- Roley Fraser
- Eddie Gillanders

Proof reading - Wendy Frazier

All Copyright - Andy Frazier 2020

Jack Dick

This book is the first print of this story about Jack Dick. Although based mainly on real life events, some of the details may have been embellished in the lack of actual facts. However, after 2 years of research the author believes it to be an accurate account of his life.

The author is currently working on a screen-script for this story.

For any comments or enquiries, please Contact andyfrazier@hotmail.co.uk

Or visit www.andyfrazier.co.uk

Printed in the USA
CPSIA information can be obtained
at www.ICGtesting.com
LVHW010202290524
781608LV00001B/190